PRAYERS &
DECLARATIONS
THAT OPEN THE
COURTS OF
HEAVEN

Destiny Image books by
Robert Henderson

Receiving Healing from the Courts of Heaven

*Unlocking Destinies From the Courts
of Heaven Curriculum*

Unlocking Destinies From the Courts of Heaven

Operating in the Courts of Heaven

PRAYERS &
DECLARATIONS
THAT OPEN THE
COURTS OF
HEAVEN

ROBERT
HENDERSON

DESTINY IMAGE® PUBLISHERS, INC.
P.O. Box 310, Shippensburg, PA 17257-0310
"Promoting Inspired Lives."

This book and all other Destiny Image and Destiny Image Fiction books are available at Christian bookstores and distributors worldwide.

Cover design by Eileen Rockwell

For more information on foreign distributors, call 717-532-3040.

Or reach us on the Internet: www.destinyimage.com

ISBN 13 HC: 978-0-7684-1869-9
ISBN 13 TP: 978-0-7684-1888-0
ISBN LP: 978-0-7684-4809-2
ISBN 13 eBook: 978-0-7684-1870-5

For Worldwide Distribution, Printed in the U.S.A.

5 6 7 8 / 22 21 20 19

Table of Contents

CHAPTER 1

PRESENTING CASES IN THE COURTS OF HEAVEN

A S I have sought to progress in the Courts of Heaven, I have gleaned ideas and concepts to approach this realm. This has been and continues to be one of the greatest thrills of my life. I have for many years had a heart for prayer. God has graciously taught me many things as I have endeavored to be more effective. The Courts of Heaven, however, has been without question the single most important revelation I have received. This insight has caused me to understand *dimensions of the spirit* I had no concept of before. This began to come into view as I saw that Jesus placed prayer in three distinct realms. When the disciples asked Jesus to teach them to pray, in Luke chapter 11 and then in Luke chapter 18, Jesus revealed three dimensions from which we can pray. He spoke of approaching God as Father (see Luke 11:2). He then spoke of approaching God as Friend (see Luke 11:5–8). In Luke 18:1–8, Jesus then placed prayer in a judicial system where we must approach God as Judge. Judges, of course, rule over judicial systems and *courts*. There is a very real *Court* in heaven that we have been given the right to approach. Daniel 7:10 gives one of the clearest pictures of this spiritual dimension.

> *A fiery stream issued*
> *And came forth from before Him.*
> *A thousand thousands ministered to Him;*
> *Ten thousand times ten thousand stood before Him.*
> *The court was seated,*
> *And the books were opened.*

When we examine these scriptures and others, we find what the Bible is calling *The Court* here is referred to in other portions of Scripture. Sometimes it is called the Throne. Still in other passages we see the activity surrounding this spiritual dimension called *The Court*. The bottom line is that we have been given the right, privilege, and even responsibility to function here. Hebrews 12:22–24 gives us insight into this realm.

But you have come to Mount Zion and to the city of the living God, the heavenly Jerusalem, to an innumerable company of angels, to the general assembly and church of the firstborn who are registered in heaven, to God the Judge of all, to the spirits of just men made perfect, to Jesus the Mediator of the new covenant, and to the blood of sprinkling that speaks better things than that of Abel.

The New Testament writer of the book of Hebrews says *we have come* to a place in the spirit we need to recognize. We are in a spiritual arena where the Courts of Heaven operate. We know this because we *have come* to God the Judge of all. In the spiritual sphere described here, we should learn to pray prayers from a judicial viewpoint. This can be very effective in the Courts of Heaven.

To understand this, we should see another scripture where the Courts of Heaven are spoken of and insight is given to their operations. Revelation 12:10–11 unveils some secrets about this dimension.

Then I heard a loud voice saying in heaven, "Now salvation, and strength, and the kingdom of our God, and the power of His Christ have come, for the

> *accuser of our brethren, who accused them before our*
> *God day and night, has been cast down. And they*
> *overcame him by the blood of the Lamb and by the*
> *word of their testimony, and they did not love their*
> *lives to the death."*

The word "accuser" is the Greek word "kategoros," and it means a complainant at law or in a legal system. It is speaking of one who is bringing a case against you that is legal in nature. It is not talking of someone speaking evil against you in the natural world. The Bible says it is *before our God*. This means these are voices and words from someone in the spirit world seeking to deny us breakthroughs and all Jesus died for us to have. This is why so often we do not see everything Jesus died for us to have becoming functionally ours. We need to know how to answer the accuser's case against us and silence his demands. When we do, we will gain all that belongs to us that Jesus's sacrifice has secured. This scripture not only describes the problem and conflict, it also gives us the answer to it. We overcome any and all cases against us by *the blood of the Lamb, the word of our testimony, and loving not our lives unto death*. These are three essentials to receiving breakthroughs for our life.

The *blood of the Lamb* is how we undo the cases against us. The accuser, the devil, uses our violations, sins, transgressions, and iniquities as legal elements to bring cases against us. In Hebrews 12:24, we are told we have come to the *blood that speaks*. This is an important scripture. We must come,

> *To Jesus the Mediator of the new covenant, and to the*
> *blood of sprinkling that speaks better things than that*
> *of Abel.*

Notice that Jesus's blood is speaking better things than what Abel's blood spoke. We must remember this is a reference to Cain killing Abel in Genesis 4:8–12. In these verses we see the blood of Abel calling out to God for judgment.

> *Now Cain talked with Abel his brother; and it came*
> *to pass, when they were in the field, that Cain rose up*
> *against Abel his brother and killed him.*
>
> *Then the Lord said to Cain, "Where is Abel your*
> *brother?"*
>
> *He said, "I do not know. Am I my brother's keeper?"*
>
> *And He said, "What have you done? The voice of*
> *your brother's blood cries out to Me from the ground.*
> *So now you are cursed from the earth, which has*

*opened its mouth to receive your brother's blood from
your hand. When you till the ground, it shall no longer
yield its strength to you. A fugitive and a vagabond
you shall be on the earth."*

The testimony of Abel's blood before the Courts of
Heaven caused God as Judge to pass sentence on Cain. The
good news is that the blood of Jesus is speaking *better things*
for us. Jesus's blood is crying out for mercy, redemption, and
forgiveness. The blood of Jesus is granting God the legal
right He needs to forgive us and cleanse us of all our sins,
transgressions, and iniquities. This is why First John 1:9
tells us that if we *confess* our sins, He is faithful and just to
forgive and cleanse.

*If we confess our sins, He is faithful and just to forgive
us our sins and to cleanse us from all unrighteousness.*

Every legal mandate has been met through the blood and
body of Jesus as our sacrifice for sin. Every legality by which
God needs to be able to forgive us has been met. When we
confess, we are agreeing with this legal action of Jesus's sacrifice. The word *confess* is the Greek word "homologeo," and
it means "to say the same thing." It also means to "release
corroborating testimony in a legal system." When I *confess*

my sins, transgressions, and iniquities, I am agreeing with what heaven says about them. I therefore get the benefit of what the blood of Jesus is saying on my behalf. My confession brings me into agreement with the "speaking blood of Jesus." I am agreeing with the blood of Jesus's testimony. I get the full benefits of what Jesus died for me to have. Any and every case and accusation against me is now dismissed because of His blood! Every case against me is revoked and removed. This is what Colossians 2:14 is declaring. God forgave us,

> *Having wiped out the handwriting of requirements that was against us, which was contrary to us. And He has taken it out of the way, having nailed it to the cross.*

The "*handwriting of requirements that was against us*" is a reference to the devil's case against us. He takes advantage of the law and word of God and builds cases against me. Jesus's death on the cross on our behalf takes all of this away. He legally answered it all. When I *confess* and agree with what Jesus has done legally, I get the full effects of His work for me in my life. Through the blood, I overcome any and every accusation the devil brings against me and every legal right he claims to have to devour me. I overcome his case against me by the blood of the Lamb!

The next thing mentioned in Revelation 12:11 is the *word of our testimony*. The blood of Jesus nullifies any of the devil's cases against us. This is essential to any legal endeavor. Any case against us has to be removed. However, a judge cannot render a verdict on our behalf just because a case against us is dismissed. It's one thing to be found not guilty. We still need a case presented on our behalf to get what belongs to us. He also needs a case presented in its stead. This is what occurs through the *word of our testimony*. This is the presentation of our own case. I want to zero in on one main way to present our own case before the Courts of Heaven. This is essential to getting answers we desire from His Courts.

We must present our case from the books/scrolls of heaven. Daniel 7:10 connects the books of heaven with the Courts of Heaven.

> *A fiery stream issued*
> *And came forth from before Him.*
> *A thousand thousands ministered to Him;*
> *Ten thousand times ten thousand stood before Him.*
> *The court was seated,*
> *And the books were opened.*

Notice that as the Court comes to order and is in session, books are open. There are many books in heaven. One of the main books, however, is what I call *books of destiny*. Psalm 139:16 gives us some insight into these books/scrolls.

> *Your eyes saw my substance, being yet unformed.*
> *And in Your book they all were written,*
> *The days fashioned for me,*
> *When as yet there were none of them.*

This verse says God wrote down my substance and my days in a book. Notice God wrote down what He saw about me. God prophetically saw what I was to be. So, what is in my book is my prophetic destiny and purpose for being alive on earth. When the Bible refers to *my substance*, it is speaking of my DNA. It is talking about what makes me who I am. It is talking about my likes and dislikes. It is speaking of my gifting and abilities. It is referring to what I'm good at and not good at. This is essential because these preferences and abilities have to line up with the purpose I was created to fulfill. This means my desires will be in agreement with what I was made to accomplish. My gifts will be consistent with what is necessary to fulfill my destiny and purpose. To discover our prophetic destiny and purpose, we should then pay attention to our innate desires. These can be significant clues to uncovering what we exist for. Notice also that before I lived any days on earth they were written down for me. This means that the length of my life was determined before I ever existed. How long I would live and what I am to accomplish was determined and written in my book in heaven. I also believe that *days fashioned for me* refers to God's timing. The Bible doesn't say years or even months. The Bible pinpoints days. There are certain things that God mandates for certain junctures of our lives. These things must happen at these times, otherwise the purpose of our lives can be thrown off-kilter. We must sense this timing and began to agree with it from heaven. Otherwise the devil will seek to disrupt God's timing so that what is written in our books cannot fully occur. Our prayers before the Courts of Heaven must address anything the devil would use to interrupt the timing of God. Daniel 7:25–26 shows the devil's forces seeking to change timing.

> *He shall speak pompous words against the Most High,*
> *Shall persecute the saints of the Most High,*
> *And shall intend to change times and law.*
> *Then the saints shall be given into his hand*
> *For a time and times and half a time.*

But the court shall be seated,
And they shall take away his dominion,
To consume and destroy it forever.

Notice that the devil's will to change timing allows the saints to fall into demonic hands. Notice, however, it is the Courts of Heaven that undo this attempt. The ruling from the Courts of Heaven causes the disruption of the devil's timing and allows things to be reset according to God! We must know how to go before the Courts of Heaven and reset the timing of our divine purposes. These purposes have been written in the books of heaven. They are supposed to occur. The devil, however, wants to stop them or at least delay them so their impact is not complete. The reason is because the devil realizes that God's purposes are connected to the fulfillment of our destinies. God has a purpose to fulfill on the earth through us. Ephesians 1:11 tells us that our predestined reason for existence is connected to God's purpose.

In Him also we have obtained an inheritance, being
predestined according to the purpose of Him who
works all things according to the counsel of His will.

Predestination simply means there was a plan for our lives that was written in a book before we ever existed. Ephesians 2:10 clearly shows this truth and verifies it.

> *For we are His workmanship, created in Christ Jesus*
> *for good works, which God prepared beforehand that*
> *we should walk in them.*

Notice that we are the creation and workmanship of God. This means we declare the Artist's character, ability, and thought process. We were made for His glory. Individually, each of us was created for certain good works that were planned and prepared *beforehand*. So we are here on earth to fulfill what was planned for us before we existed. Literally this happened before time began. Second Timothy 1:9 tells us this. It is God,

> *Who has saved us and called us with a holy calling,*
> *not according to our works, but according to His own*
> *purpose and grace which was given to us in Christ*
> *Jesus before time began.*

Purpose and grace were apportioned to us before time began. We have been in the mind and heart of God always.

We are here on the earth to discover what we were made for and to fulfill it. This doesn't mean we are forced to do this. It is our job to discover the reason for being alive in this time and place. The sad truth is that most people on the planet will never come into their destiny that was written in the book. They will merely exist. This greatly grieves the heart of God. He created each of us to live life and live it abundantly (see John 10:10). I believe God mourns over those who never discover the real reason for being alive on earth. Remember that God also needs us to live out what is in our book of destiny so His purposes can be completed in this realm. This is why the devil wants to keep us out of our destiny. If he can thwart enough of us from fulfilling our destiny, he can frustrate the purposes of God on the earth. This is why he seeks to disrupt God's timing in our lives. When he is able to do this, he can delay the purpose and will of God. This forces God to raise up another generation who will fulfill His will. Very much like what occurred with the children of Israel when the first group would not believe and obey God, God had to wait for another generation to arise. This delayed the plans of God from happening according to His original timing. Numbers 14:31–33 chronicles the decision of God to choose the next generation to fulfill His word.

> *But your little ones, whom you said would be victims,*
> *I will bring in, and they shall know the land which you*
> *have despised. But as for you, your carcasses shall fall*
> *in this wilderness. And your sons shall be shepherds in*
> *the wilderness forty years, and bear the brunt of your*
> *infidelity, until your carcasses are consumed in the*
> *wilderness.*

God let one generation die away because they would not believe and cooperate with His purposes. It delayed the purpose of God from being accomplished for a whole generation. God had to have a generation arise who would believe Him, take Him at His word, and see His promises fulfilled. They walked in the destiny the previous generation despised. As they did, the purposes of God were fulfilled through them. We must resist demonic attempts to disrupt the timing of our destiny and God's purposes. When we do, we can receive what has been written in the books of heaven before time began. We will deal with this whole disruption of timing in a later chapter.

Remember that our cases before the Courts of Heaven are presented from the books of heaven. We literally come before the Courts and remind God of what He wrote in the books concerning us. Isaiah 43:26 clearly defines this for us.

Put Me in remembrance;
Let us contend together;
State your case, that you may be acquitted.

Notice that when we put God in remembrance or tell Him what he wrote in our book, we are stating a case before His Courts. This is the primary way we come before the Courts of Heaven. This is why the *Court was seated and the books were open* (see Daniel 7:10). We present before His Courts our understanding of the prophetic destiny for which He made us. We ask Him for our destiny before His Courts. This requires that we have a sense of what is in our books and why we are on earth. Once we present our case, the accuser will seek to resist us receiving what we have requested. When the verse declares "Let us contend together," it means that God and us in tandem will answer any argument the devil might present. Once he is silenced and rebuffed by the blood speaking on our behalf, God is free to bring us into our destiny.

Let me give you some hints on how to discern what is written about you in the books of heaven. You cannot present a case before the Courts of Heaven without some understanding of the prophetic destiny written in your book in heaven. First of all, be mindful of the promises of God's word that apply to us all. For instance, we are promised healing, prosperity, family, harmony, and other precious things. Second Peter 1:3–4 speaks of the precious promises given to us.

His divine power has given to us all things that pertain to life and godliness, through the knowledge of Him who called us by glory and virtue, by which have been given to us exceedingly great and precious promises, that through these you may be partakers of the divine nature, having escaped the corruption that is in the world through lust.

The precious promises are given to us when we partake of His divine nature and escape the corruption of lust. The word corruption means to decay, shrivel, and wither. If we live out of lust, this is what occurs. But we have been granted the nature of God in us through the new birth. This nature delivers us from lust. As a result of God's nature in us, we have access to all the precious promises of God. We can bring these promises before the Courts and ask for what is ours by the new birth to be granted.

Another hint to discovering what is in our books in heaven is to pay attention to what we have heard personally from the Lord. If we are spending time with the Lord in prayer, meditation, and devotion, we will hear His whisper. Just like Elijah recognized God in the still, small voice, so we will hear Him. First Kings 19:12–13 references this still, small voice.

> *And after the earthquake a fire, but the* LORD *was not in the fire; and after the fire a still small voice.*
>
> *So it was, when Elijah heard it, that he wrapped his face in his mantle and went out and stood in the entrance of the cave. Suddenly a voice came to him, and said, "What are you doing here, Elijah?"*

If we were to read the entire passage here of Elijah's encounter with God, you would find he witnessed a wind, earthquake, and fire. God was in none of these. Then, this still, small voice came. This was God. God questioned Elijah as to why he was where he was. This wasn't his destiny. Many times when we get off the course of our destiny, God has to come and question us. He questions us for the purpose of reestablishing us in our destiny. In essence, God was saying to Elijah, "Why are you here? This isn't what I made you for." The Lord then gave him very detailed assignments to fulfill. He began to pull Elijah back into his destiny and what was written in his book in heaven. If we are to reach our destiny, we must listen to the still, small voice of God. In this voice will be direction and adjustment, of course, but it will always be consistent with our book in heaven. We must learn to take what we hear from the still, small voice of God and present it to the Courts of Heaven. These will be petitions we present in the Courts for us to have all that is written in our book.

We should also pay attention to prophetic words spoken over us. These words about our future, when spoken in truth, come from the books in heaven. Prophetic revelation comes from open books in heaven. This is what Isaiah 29:10–11 is referring to. In this passage, no prophetic revelation is possible because books are sealed and shut.

> *For the LORD has poured out on you*
> *The spirit of deep sleep,*
> *And has closed your eyes, namely, the prophets;*
> *And He has covered your heads, namely, the seers.*
>
> *The whole vision has become to you like the words of*
> *a book that is sealed, which men deliver to one who is*
> *literate, saying, "Read this, please." And he says, "I*
> *cannot, for it is sealed."*

When books are shut, we must see them opened to be able to prophetically present our cases before the *Courts of Heaven*. Remember that when the Court is seated the books are then opened (see Daniel 7:10). Books in heaven must be opened for the Courts of Heaven to function on our behalf. If the books are not open, we are simply telling heaven our good ideas and not presenting cases consistent with our prophetic destiny. Suffice it to say that we should cry out to God until the books of destiny are open. We will know when they are open because a sense of prophetic destiny will begin to overtake us. From this prophetic destiny, we begin to bring our case before the Courts of Heaven. The opening of these books will also allow prophetic words to be spoken over our lives by others. It is amazing to find that when our book in heaven is open, we will receive prophetic words from people concerning our divine destiny. Once we receive these prophetic words, we should present them before the Courts of Heaven. This is one of the ways we bring cases about our destiny to the Lord. The prophetic word spoken over us helps us know how to *put God in remembrance* of what He has written about us in heaven. This allows the Lord to render to us that which was written about us before time began.

A final way to discern what is written in our books in heaven is to pay attention to what stirs your heart. Desires and longings can be very real indicators of what God created you for. Again, Psalm 139:16 says *"my substance yet unformed"* was written in my book in heaven. In other words, what God wrote in my book causes me to have desires, longings, and stirrings in my heart today. It causes me to gravitate toward certain things in life. This is why we should pay attention to these desires. They are very strong clues of what is written in my book. They should not be disregarded but examined for divine influence. They very well may contain strong evidence of why I exist on this earth today. If I discern they are a part of my destiny, I should use them to present cases in the Courts of Heaven. This can be very significant to unlocking the destiny for which I was made.

The third thing spoken of in Revelation 12:11 is that to function in the Courts of Heaven is to *"love not our lives to the death."* One of the main things that grants us authority in the Courts of Heaven is to lay down our lives. In other words, we *take up our cross and follow Jesus.* In Hebrews 11:39, we see what gives us status in the Courts.

> *And all these, having obtained a good testimony through faith, did not receive the promise.*

In speaking of all the people of faith, this scripture declares they obtained a *good testimony*. This is a reference to those who served faithfully on the earth and are now in the Great Cloud of Witnesses. If you were to read the next verse, you would see that they need us to fulfill what remains so they can have their full reward. Their willingness to surrender their life to God's will has given them this place in heaven. This means they were granted status before the Courts of Heaven by virtue of the lives they lived. They, by faith, chose the ways of the Lord rather than their own ways. The result of this was a place of great influence and authority in the spirit realm. Jesus spoke of this as well. He said if we choose to follow Him and walk in His paths, we will be granted a place with Him in the spirit. Luke 9:23–24 tells us what is required of us.

> *Then He said to them all, "If anyone desires to come after Me, let him deny himself, and take up his cross daily, and follow Me. For whoever desires to save his life will lose it, but whoever loses his life for My sake will save it."*

The more we choose to obey the Lord and His word rather than our own fleshly impulses, the more we qualify to carry great authority in His Courts. We obtain for ourselves

a status in the Courts of Heaven from which we can petition the Court to see His will done on earth. The grace of
the Lord is sufficient to empower us to walk in these ways.

These three issues are paramount to praying, decreeing,
and releasing declarations in the Courts of Heaven. We
use the *blood* to silence the case against us. We present our
case through the *word of our testimony*. We obtain places
of status in the Courts by *loving not our lives to the death*.
We should make these issues part of our petition before the
Courts of Heaven as we approach this dimension.

As we proceed in our prayers, decrees, and declarations
in the Courts of Heaven, here is a prayer to approach the
Courts with these three realms in mind.

Lord, I come before Your Courts. As I stand
before You, I honor You as the Great Judge
of all and the Judge of all the earth. I thank
You for the blood of Jesus that is speaking
for me according to Hebrews 12:24. I repent of all
sins, transgressions, and iniquities that would allow
accusations against me. I thank You that the blood
is silencing every voice against me according to
Colossians 2:14. All the handwriting of ordinances
that would speak against me are now silenced by

the blood of Jesus. Thank You that all cases against me in the spirit realm are removed by virtue of who Jesus is and what He has done for me.

As I stand before Your Courts, I also present my own case before You. Your word in Isaiah 43:26 declares:

> *Put Me in remembrance;*
> *Let us contend together;*
> *State your case, that you may be acquitted.*

Lord, I place You in remembrance of what You wrote about me in my book of destiny. I thank You that I was planned and created with a divine purpose recorded in this book. I bring this purpose to you. I state my case before You. (At this point, begin to present the details of what you presently understand about your destiny.) Lord, I am asking before Your Courts that there would be a fulfillment of all that is written in my book. I repent for any place I have walked contrary to what is in my book. I am now surrendering to You and asking that the purpose of my life recorded in my book would be fulfilled. I ask for divine favor to come over my life so that the right people will help me. I ask that circumstances would line up to allow what is written in my book to be done. I ask that great doors of opportunity would open so that I might fulfill what is in my book. Lord, I ask this not just so I can be blessed and influential, but so Your divine purposes might be accomplished. Lord, I am asking that the passion of Your heart would be done through me on this earth. Let me fulfill what is in my book so the part of Your purpose I am to accomplish will happen.

Lord, I also come before Your Courts to lay my life down. I choose Your desires over my own. According to Your Word in Revelation 12:11, I love not my life to the death. I may not need to die naturally, but I choose to "die" to my own wants and wishes where they conflict with Yours. I take up my cross and follow hard after You. Lord, as I do this by Your grace, may I obtain before this Court a "good testimony." As I by faith walk in obedience to You, may I be recognized and remembered in the Courts of Heaven. May I be allowed to present cases before You on behalf of my life and my family. More importantly, Lord, may I be able to present cases for Your divine passions to be fulfilled. I lay my life before You and ask for Your grace that empowers me to obey. In Jesus's name, Amen.

CHAPTER 2

DISCERNMENT AND THE COURTS OF HEAVEN

WHEN we function in the Courts of Heaven, we must always do this through the power of the Holy Spirit. One of the tendencies we have when wanting to deal with the legalities the devil might be using against us is to become legalistic. People hear my story of how things were dealt with before the Courts of Heaven, and when I tell how I discerned that something in my bloodline was legally being used by the devil to devour and destroy me, they become obsessed with discovering any similar issue in their bloodline. This can lead to a frantic search that becomes legalistic. I do believe there are things the devil can be legally using against us. However, I believe the Holy Spirit must help us discern them.

Galatians 3:10 tells us that when we live under the law or as legalist, we come under a curse.

> *For as many as are of the works of the law are under the curse; for it is written, "Cursed is everyone who does not continue in all things which are written in the book of the law, to do them."*

Any effort on our own to obtain righteousness can actually bring us under this curse. This is because the devil is a legalist himself. When we intentionally or unintentionally begin to be justified by our works, we step back under the law. This grants the devil the *legal right* to afflict us with the curse. We are not to be living under the law as legalists but under the law of the Spirit. Romans 8:2–4 shows us that we are not to keep rules, regulations, and rituals but rather to be under the governance of the Spirit.

> *For the law of the Spirit of life in Christ Jesus has made me free from the law of sin and death. For what the law could not do in that it was weak through the flesh, God did by sending His own Son in the likeness of sinful flesh, on account of sin: He condemned sin in the flesh, that the righteous requirement of the law*

> *might be fulfilled in us who do not walk according to*
> *the flesh but according to the Spirit.*

We are, by the power of the Holy Spirit, to fulfill the righteous requirements of the law. In other words, we are to accomplish what the law intended to do. Through our empowerment by the Spirit of God, we manifest God's righteousness on the earth. We do this not by keeping rules but by following the leadership of the Spirit in our lives. Galatians 5:16–18 refers to this truth as well.

> *I say then: Walk in the Spirit, and you shall not fulfill*
> *the lust of the flesh. For the flesh lusts against the*
> *Spirit, and the Spirit against the flesh; and these are*
> *contrary to one another, so that you do not do the*
> *things that you wish. But if you are led by the Spirit,*
> *you are not under the law.*

Notice that walking in the Spirit gives us authority to overcome the lust of the flesh. As we come under the authority and rulership of the Holy Spirit, He takes control of our desires, appetites, and longings. As a result, we fulfill the demands of the law by the Holy Spirit's power. We don't, however, do this by keeping rules and regulations. We do this through coming under the *law* of the Spirit.

We get free from the law of sin and death by surrendering ourselves to another law. This is called the *law of the Spirit of Life* as I previously mentioned. The Bible never gives us permission to be lawless. We are simply exchanging the law of sin and death that could never produce real righteousness for the law of the Spirit of Life that can. This means the Spirit must lead us. The Holy Spirit will work in us to complete the will of God. This is what Jesus was speaking of in John 16:7–11.

> *Nevertheless I tell you the truth. It is to your advantage that I go away; for if I do not go away, the Helper will not come to you; but if I depart, I will send Him to you. And when He has come, He will convict the world of sin, and of righteousness, and of judgment: of sin, because they do not believe in Me, of righteousness, because I go to My Father and you see Me no more; of judgment, because the ruler of this world is judged.*

In verse 10 especially, we see Jesus showing that the Holy Spirit would convict and convince them of righteousness. Jesus said the Holy Spirit would show them what real righteousness was. He would no longer be among them for them to watch Him in the flesh. However, the Spirit would convince them of the standard of righteousness that the Father desired. I like to put it this way: The Spirit keeps us out of the ditches of lawlessness and legalism and on the pathway of righteousness. There are the two extremes we tend to fall into. In our efforts to be righteous, we can tend toward legalism. In our efforts to be free in the Spirit, I have watched people become lawless and consider it okay. Both of these extremes lead to death in the spirit. The letter kills, Paul said in Second Corinthians 3:6. It is God,

> *Who also made us sufficient as ministers of the new covenant, not of the letter but of the Spirit; for the letter kills, but the Spirit gives life.*

This means that trying to keep the letter of the law will bring failure and lifelessness. There is never a law that can give life. Simultaneously, lawlessness or living without law also brings death. Romans 8:4–6 gives us insight into what occurs when we throw off the restraints of the Holy Spirit. It says that God sent His Son so,

> *That the righteous requirement of the law might be fulfilled in us who do not walk according to the flesh but according to the Spirit. For those who live according to the flesh set their minds on the things of the flesh, but*

those who live according to the Spirit, the things of the
Spirit. For to be carnally minded is death, but to be
spiritually minded is life and peace.

To be able to fulfill the righteous requirement that the law desired, we must do it under the constraints of the Spirit. If we, however, begin to live according to the flesh or our carnal yearnings and desires, we will find death. So both legalism and lawlessness end in death. Only by living under the constraints and freedom of the Holy Spirit do we escape these things. When we are under the law or governance of the Spirit and His control, we will know His freedom but also His restraints. This will result in true righteousness.

This is what the Apostle Paul was speaking of when he talked of liberty and freedom. He was not speaking of our need to jump around in a worship service, although there is nothing wrong with that. He was speaking of being liberated from the restraints of the law because we had come under the higher law of the Spirit. Second Corinthians 3:17–18 declares what the Lordship of Jesus does through the Holy Spirit.

Now the Lord is the Spirit; and where the Spirit of
the Lord is, there is liberty. But we all, with unveiled

face, beholding as in a mirror the glory of the Lord, are being transformed into the same image from glory to glory, just as by the Spirit of the Lord.

Notice that the Lord Jesus executes His Lordship through the Holy Spirit. Paul says when we are under the authority of the Spirit, we are at liberty. We are free from the law of condemnation. We are free to be transformed into the glorious image of the Lord and His glory. This would mean His character, life, power, and spirit. We are fashioned into His image and likeness. This is not occurring because we are keeping the law but because we are living in the freedom and constraints of the Holy Spirit. Paul addresses this again in Galatians 5:11–13.

And I, brethren, if I still preach circumcision, why do I still suffer persecution? Then the offense of the cross has ceased. I could wish that those who trouble you would even cut themselves off!

For you, brethren, have been called to liberty; only do not use liberty as an opportunity for the flesh, but through love serve one another.

Paul desires those who are trying to bring the Galatians back under the law be cut off. He then declares, "You have been called to liberty." They and we are free from the restraints of the law. Then, he makes this statement: "Only do not use it as an opportunity for the flesh." In other words, don't live in sin and unrighteousness. Don't be unloving and unkind to people. Serve them instead. Live under the rule of the Spirit and fulfill the law's intent through His power. This is the real liberty and freedom to which we have been called.

With all this said, what does this mean in regards to functioning in the Courts of Heaven? For me, this means I, by faith, need to establish before the Courts my legal standing based on what Jesus has done. In other words, I declare I am not justified by the law, but by faith in Jesus and His grace. I establish that I am not under the law but governed by the Spirit of God. The Spirit of God determines my activities and functions. I claim all that Jesus died for me to have. This has great power in the Courts. Having said this, the iniquity that is associated with my bloodline will try to exercise its influence over me. To be freed from this influence and any legal issue the devil would raise, I will need to bring this before the Courts of Heaven and repent of it. Even when I do this, I am exercising faith and confidence in what Jesus did on the cross for me. I am forcibly removing any legal right with which the devil might try to resist me.

As I seek to discern anything in my bloodline being used legally against me, ultimately my dependence is on the revelation through the Holy Spirit. I use any natural knowledge I have of my bloodline. I use any prophetic insight granted to me. I pay attention to instructions given me through dreams, visions, and other spiritual encounters. However, when I have dealt with anything I have perceived, I simply trust the Lord. I do not go on a *witch hunt*. I do not become *paranoid* and look for *the thing*. This will not produce anything healthy. In all my functioning in the Courts of Heaven, I have never done this. If there were something God needed to let me know, then He would reveal it to me. I live by Philippians 3:15.

> *Therefore let us, as many as are mature, have this mind; and if in anything you think otherwise, God will reveal even this to you.*

I seek to walk as a mature believer. My prayer is that if there is something I'm not seeing, that the Holy Spirit will show me. God will reveal to me anything that would be hindering my maturity and fullness in Him. I have confidence and trust in the Lord. I do not have to frantically search or become a legalist to discover it. Anything I need to know God will reveal to me.

Here is a prayer to help live as one led by the Spirit and not as a legalist that can be put under a curse.

> Lord, I by faith come to stand before Your Courts. Thank You that I have the right to stand in this place. Lord, I come and stand here as one trusting in all that Jesus has done for me. Any condemnation, shame, or guilt resulting from living under the law, I repent of. I can never be good enough myself. I trust in Your goodness for me.
>
> Lord, as I stand here, I thank You that the law of the Spirit of Life has set me free from all the condemnation of the law of sin and death. I now live under the freedom of the Spirit but also the restraints of the Spirit as well. I submit myself to the Lordship of Jesus executed through the person of the Holy Spirit. I surrender my life to the rulership of the Spirit of God. I ask that any curse brought about through any legalistic attitude in me would now be dismissed. I thank You that its power is broken and

its authority to operate against me is now removed. Thank You, Lord, so much for this.

As I yield to the Holy Spirit's governance, I ask that anything in my bloodline that the devil would be using legally against me would be revealed. I repent for any effort of my own to discover these things through frantic search or paranoia. I trust You, Lord, to reveal these things to me and bring me to maturity. As I come out from under the law and into the freedom of the Spirit, I am open, through whatever means You desire, to receive these revelations. I ask, Lord, that these things might be known through the power of the Holy Spirit. If there is any legal thing working against me in the spirit, please let it be known to me. I trust You. Lord, and the precious Spirit of God to unveil this. In Jesus's holy name, Amen.

CHAPTER 3

THE HOLY SPIRIT – OUR LEGAL AID

A S I have written several books on the Courts of Heaven, revealing this dimension of prayer, people have asked for prayers to pray in this realm. At first, I was reluctant to provide such a thing. I felt that it is the Holy Spirit that empowers us to pray in this place of the spirit. Romans 8:26 tell us it is the Spirit that helps us where we are weak and have no ability.

Likewise the Spirit also helps in our weaknesses. For we do not know what we should pray for as we ought, but the Spirit Himself makes intercession for us with groanings which cannot be uttered.

It is the person of the Holy Spirit who shows us how to pray. In fact, when we understand who the Holy Spirit is, as Jesus taught us, we discover He is our legal aid. John 14:26 is one of the places where Jesus refers to this function of the Spirit.

> *But the Helper, the Holy Spirit, whom the Father will send in My name, He will teach you all things, and bring to your remembrance all things that I said to you.*

The word "Helper" is the Greek word "parakletos." It means a comforter or an advocate. An advocate is someone in a legal system who speaks on our behalf. This same Greek word is used to describe Jesus's function in First John 2:1.

> *My little children, these things I write to you, so that you may not sin. And if anyone sins, we have an Advocate with the Father, Jesus Christ the righteous.*

Again the word "advocate" is the Greek word "parakletos." This is the same word used to describe the Holy Spirit. So Jesus through the Holy Spirit is standing as our advocate. The Holy Spirit is taking all that Jesus has done and is doing and is functionally applying it to our lives. He is helping us to know how to pray according to the will of God and, in fact, is praying through us in agreement with God's passion. When the Holy Spirit empowers our prayers, He gives us the wisdom to know how to plead our case in the Courts of Heaven. Sometimes the Holy Spirit does this through what we refer to as our prayer language. The Bible says the Spirit empowers us to pray in "the spirit or in tongues." First Corinthians 14:2 tells us that when we speak in tongues, we are speaking to God. This is prayer.

> *For he who speaks in a tongue does not speak to men but to God, for no one understands him; however, in the spirit he speaks mysteries.*

Our prayer language, or tongues, releases mysteries. This means, among other things, that we may not exactly know what we are saying. We know by faith, however, that we are praying according to the will of God. The word "mysteries" is the Greek word "musterion." This word means to shut the mouth, such as silence imposed on those initiated into a religious rite. I take this to mean that as one who prays in the Spirit, I am invited into a secret place and can discern secret things from the Lord. I am an initiated one. I am granted entrance into spiritual dimensions through my prayer language. My prayer language allows me to move into these realms of the spirit where others are not allowed. This is not for a special few, but it is for those who have received the infilling of the Holy Spirit and pray in tongues. This "secret place" in the spirit can involve the Courts of Heaven. This is a spiritual dimension where things legally are set in order for divine breakthroughs.

Many times when I am approaching the Courts of Heaven, I just come with my prayer language. I understand that the Spirit of God is acting as my legal aid, making intercession according to the will of God. In addition, sometimes the Spirit will cause "groaning" of deep intercession to come. This is not just praying in tongues. These can be deep travails of the Spirit moving through us, interceding for us before the Courts of Heaven. Romans 8:23 tells us as a result of receiving the Holy Spirit, there is a groaning that can come.

Not only that, but we also who have the firstfruits of the Spirit, even we ourselves groan within ourselves, eagerly waiting for the adoption, the redemption of our body.

The adoption or redemption of our bodies signifies the day of resurrection when the dead in Christ shall rise (see 1 Thessalonians 4:16). The Bible is connecting the groaning and travailing within us to this climatic event. Literally, even this event will not occur without the groaning of the prayers of the saints, which birth it. There is a groaning that is necessary to birth the coming of the Lord and the resurrection from the dead. Many believe this is just a sovereign act of God. However, when you piece Scripture together, it appears our prayer life in the Spirit gives birth to this culmination of the age. I simply cite this to make us aware that deep prayer in the Spirit is necessary for everything God will do on earth, including the resurrection of the dead. May we go deeper into the realms of prayer so that God's purposes can occur!

Another way the Holy Spirit operates as our legal aid in the Courts of Heaven is by granting us wisdom and understanding from which we can pray. We must have this knowledge to present our cases to the Courts of Heaven effectively. Ephesians 1:15–17 tells us that Paul cried out to God for this wisdom and revelation.

> *Therefore I also, after I heard of your faith in the Lord Jesus and your love for all the saints, do not cease to give thanks for you, making mention of you in my prayers: that the God of our Lord Jesus Christ, the*

> *Father of glory, may give to you the spirit of wisdom*
> *and revelation in the knowledge of Him.*

We must have this if we are to be effective in the Courts of Heaven. First Corinthians 14:14–15 shows the order of events necessary to bring about this understanding.

> *For if I pray in a tongue, my spirit prays, but my*
> *understanding is unfruitful. What is the conclusion*
> *then? I will pray with the spirit, and I will also pray*
> *with the understanding. I will sing with the spirit, and*
> *I will also sing with the understanding.*

Notice that Paul prayed first in the spirit, then in his understanding. It was praying in the spirit that opened his understanding. It was only once he understood the spirit that he could logically and intellectually present his case in the Courts of Heaven. This has occurred with me many times. My times of prayer in the spirit have produced understanding that I could then present in the Courts. One occasion was when it seemed things were being delayed that I knew were the will of God. So often people take a passive stance toward receiving from the Lord. I have learned that often it isn't a timing issue that is delaying the promise. At times, it is a legal issue in the spirit that is being used by the enemy to stop the promise. This has been a major issue I have had to contend with in the Courts of Heaven to unlock the destiny God had for me. I have dealt significant blows in the spirit from the Courts of Heaven to undo things causing delays. I have found, however, that I must continue to be sensitive to the Spirit should I see delays. Just such a thing began to happen. As I was praying in the spirit, I became aware there were voices still speaking against me. This is what Revelation 12:10 speaks of. There is an accuser that is speaking before God's Court against us.

> *Then I heard a loud voice saying in heaven, "Now salvation, and strength, and the kingdom of our God, and the power of His Christ have come, for the accuser of our brethren, who accused them before our God day and night, has been cast down."*

As we have shared earlier, the word "accuser" is the Greek word "kategoros," and it means to be a complainant at law or in a legal system. It means to stand against someone in an assembly. So the accuser is speaking against us in the assembly of heaven or the Courts of Heaven where verdicts are rendered.

As I prayed in the spirit, I understood that there were voices against me, accusing me of taking things that didn't belong to me. The accuser, based on the complaints from those misinformed in the natural world, was making accusations against me. When people in the natural world speak evil against us, it can give the accuser ammunition. I understood this was happening to me. I needed to undo and silence any and every voice against me before the throne of God. I realized these voices were "bogging" me down and delaying the fulfillment of my promises. To fully be aware of these threats, we should understand Isaiah 54:17. This verse declares the power of words and tongues against us.

> *"No weapon formed against you shall prosper,*
> *And every tongue which rises against you in judgment*
> *You shall condemn.*
> *This is the heritage of the servants of the LORD,*
> *And their righteousness is from Me,"*
> *Says the LORD.*

A weapon against us speaks of something working against us in the natural. In other words, a situation, circumstance, health issue, financial strain, or anything resisting and complicating life in the natural realm is a weapon. Notice, however, that what is producing it is a "tongue" of judgment.

These are the words against you in the spirit realm. The problem in the natural realm is being created and driven by words of accusation in the spirit realm. If we want to remove the weapon and NOT allow it to prosper, we must silence the "tongue." This is done through the revelation of what is ours through the new birth. This verse declares that the right to silence the tongues is our heritage and our righteousness from the Lord. In other words, the Old Testament prophet is looking toward what Jesus would accomplish. Through our faith in Jesus and His work on our behalf on the cross, we are positioned in the spirit realm to undo every word that would allow the weapons to injure us. This is our heritage or birthright, and I have the "right" to stand before Him and undo and condemn every voice against me. I am accepted and permitted to stand in the Courts of Heaven and silence words of accusation against me.

This is what I was led to do as I prayed in the spirit. I understood these words had to be dealt with if the delay against me was going to be removed. As I continued to pray in the spirit, I was drawn to Numbers 16:14–15. Moses, in speaking before the Lord, answers the accusations that Korah, a rebel, is bringing against him.

> *"Moreover you have not brought us into a land flowing with milk and honey, nor given us inheritance of*

> *fields and vineyards. Will you put out the eyes of these men? We will not come up!"*
>
> *Then Moses was very angry, and said to the LORD, "Do not respect their offering. I have not taken one donkey from them, nor have I hurt one of them."*

Korah is accusing Moses of not doing what he promised. He is attacking Moses and saying he is seeking to persuade the people to keep believing him even though he hasn't delivered on his promises. Moses then quits talking to Korah and directs his words to God the Judge. He states that he has taken nothing from them. He declares the accusation that he is plundering the people false. Moses is speaking this before the Courts of Heaven.

The Lord led me to do the same thing: to deal with the words and tongues of judgments against me. I declared, "I have taken nothing from anyone." I was aware that when I went before the Courts and made this statement, heaven would search out whether it was so or not. This was the only way to get the words silenced against me that were causing the delay. Once I did this, I asked the Courts of Heaven for these words and tongues against me to be silenced and condemned. I knew in the spirit that they were. The result was an immediate ending of the delays. Less than 12 hours later, phone calls began to come, setting in place what had been promised. I began to step into the fullness of the promises made to me. This was allowed because the voices were silenced that wanted to "bog down" what God intended and desired.

All of this happened as I was able to discern, through praying in the spirit, what was transpiring in the unseen realm. The Holy Spirit was operating as my legal aid. He was functioning as my advocate and helping me navigate the spirit dimension. You can have this as well. In fact, I believe it is virtually impossible to be effective in the Courts of Heaven without the Spirit's power. As we practice praying in the spirit, we learn more about how to pray from this realm as well (see 1 Corinthians 14:15). This is one of the main functions of praying in tongues.

Praying in tongues is a result of the infilling of the Holy Spirit. Acts 2:4 tells us decisively that tongues are a result of the Holy Spirit filling and empowering us. On Pentecost, Jesus's disciples experienced this.

And they were all filled with the Holy Spirit and began to speak with other tongues, as the Spirit gave them utterance.

To be able to pray in tongues and have our understanding opened to perceive spiritual realities, we must be filled or baptized in the Holy Spirit. This is the term John the Baptist used to describe what Jesus would do for those who believed in Him in John 1:33.

> *I did not know Him, but He who sent me to baptize*
> *with water said to me, "Upon whom you see the Spirit*
> *descending, and remaining on Him, this is He who*
> *baptizes with the Holy Spirit."*

To be baptized means to be immersed or submerged. In other words, just like water covers us in baptism, so the Spirit covers us as well. We are to be overwhelmed and under the complete influence of the Spirit. The Holy Spirit must take absolute control of us, and we must be under His complete authority. Jesus is the One who baptizes or fills us with the Spirit. God gave the Spirit to Jesus to pour out on us as a result of all He did. Acts 2:33 tells us that Jesus was granted the Spirit to give to us.

> *Therefore being exalted to the right hand of God, and*
> *having received from the Father the promise of the*
> *Holy Spirit, He poured out this which you now see*
> *and hear.*

It is the passion of Jesus to empower His followers with the Spirit. The Father gave the Holy Spirit to Jesus to give to those who belong to Him. One of the things we have seen happen once the Spirit comes is that we are empowered to pray. When the Holy Spirit comes upon us, there is an unction from which we can pray. No longer will I just pray from my natural abilities. I will be strengthened to pray out of a prophetic unction birthed by the Holy Spirit. This changes everything. Jesus desires to baptize any and all in the Holy Spirit. His work on the cross, His resurrection, ascension, and position at the right hand of the Father is so we can be filled with the Spirit. When the Holy Spirit came upon the disciples in the upper room on the day of Pentecost, it was THE SIGN that Jesus had reached heaven and was seated at God's right hand as Lord of all. In Acts 2:32–36, Peter tells us the coming of the Spirit on that day signified the leadership Jesus had been granted.

This Jesus God has raised up, of which we are all witnesses. Therefore being exalted to the right hand of God, and having received from the Father the promise of the Holy Spirit, He poured out this which you now see and hear.

For David did not ascend into the heavens, but he says himself:

> *"The LORD said to my Lord,*
> *'Sit at My right hand,*
> *Till I make Your enemies Your footstool.'"*
>
> *Therefore let all the house of Israel know assuredly*
> *that God has made this Jesus, whom you crucified,*
> *both Lord and Christ.*

They knew Jesus was seated at the Father's right hand because the anointing and power of the Holy Spirit had now come. The Holy Spirit had come to declare the Lordship and authority of Jesus on earth. He came to empower the disciples to be witnesses that God had raised Jesus up and seated Him at His right hand. When the Holy Spirit fills us, we, too, become empowered. We can pray prayers that release the kingdom on earth. Our empowerment by the Spirit moves us into realms of prayer that produce breakthrough.

As we delve deeper into prayers, decrees, declarations, and announcements in and from the Courts of Heaven, I would ask that if you haven't received this empowerment and filling and would like to, please pray this prayer in faith. As you pray, believe that the anointing of the Spirit will come. As you ask Jesus to be your baptizer in the Spirit, accept by faith this gift He obtained from the Father for you. As you pray, open your mouth and begin to speak in a language you haven't learned in the natural. Jesus said out of your innermost being will flow a river (see John 7:38–39). The Holy Spirit will ignite deep in your spirit a flow that will rush out when you open your mouth. Let the "tongues and language" of the Spirit flow through you.

Lord Jesus, I thank You for all You have done for me on the cross through Your resurrection and ascension. Thank You that You are now at the right hand of the Father. You have received from the Father the Holy Spirit and have poured Him out. I now receive from Your gracious hand the person of the Holy Spirit and my empowerment to pray. I receive the gift of tongues now in Jesus's name. (By faith, open your mouth and begin to pray in the language of the Spirit. Don't worry about what it sounds like.)

CHAPTER 4

OPERATING AS A JUDGE

BEFORE we move fully into prayer, decrees, and declarations in the Courts of Heaven, we should understand this realm from the position of a judge. Most Christians would say God is the Judge. We might, however, be surprised to find that God would allow us to operate as "judges" in the realm of the spirit as well. In fact, the whole idea of decrees and declarations emerges from this concept. Judges are those whose words change the course of events. Judges' decrees, declarations, and verdicts set things in motion that wouldn't otherwise happen. We actually can be granted this role from which these statements can be made! In Job 22:27–28, we see this idea.

You will make your prayer to Him,
He will hear you,

And you will pay your vows.
You will also declare a thing,
And it will be established for you;
So light will shine on your ways.

This verse actually says we can declare something and see it established. In other words, our words in the spirit realm cause something to happen in the natural realm. This can be because we are sitting as judges in these dimensions. When someone challenged my idea about us becoming judges, I reminded them that God actually put a book in the Bible called "Judges." It chronicles the life of both men and women who functioned as judges to set justice in place. In fact, judges were God's first choice to create and sustain order in society. Only after the people cried for a "king" did God grant them one. Before this, there were judges. We find in First Samuel 8:19–22 God giving in and granting them a king instead of judges.

Nevertheless the people refused to obey the voice of
Samuel; and they said, "No, but we will have a king
over us, that we also may be like all the nations, and
that our king may judge us and go out before us and
fight our battles."

*And Samuel heard all the words of the people, and he
repeated them in the hearing of the LORD. So the LORD
said to Samuel, "Heed their voice, and make them a
king."*

*And Samuel said to the men of Israel, "Every man go
to his city."*

Even though Samuel warned them from God what
would happen if they had a king, they still demanded it.
I am showing you this simply to make the point that this
wasn't God's ideal. God's perfect situation was judges who
were before kings. In fact, when things became corrupt
in Israel, God's solution was to restore judges. Isaiah 1:26
shows that when Jerusalem was full of wickedness and sin,
God's fix was reinstituting judges.

*I will restore your judges as at the first,
And your counselors as at the beginning.
Afterward you shall be called the city of righteousness,
the faithful city.*

God said when there were judges and counselors again,
the city would be known as a righteous and faithful place.
This is the power of judges. Righteous judges can bring

order and peace back into place. This is true in the natural but also in the spirit realm. We need righteous and just judges in the natural, but we also need them in the spirit to set things in divine order through decrees and declarations.

Jesus actually spoke of His apostles operating as judges. In Luke 22:28–30, we see Jesus promising His apostles positions as judges.

> *But you are those who have continued with Me in My trials. And I bestow upon you a kingdom, just as My Father bestowed one upon Me, that you may eat and drink at My table in My kingdom, and sit on thrones judging the twelve tribes of Israel.*

I personally do not believe this was just in the afterlife, but I believe Jesus was speaking in the spiritual dimension right now. In other words, He was promising them that because of their faithfulness, they would operate as judges. This is what Peter did in Acts 5:1–5 when he judged Ananias and then later Sapphira.

> *But a certain man named Ananias, with Sapphira his wife, sold a possession. And he kept back part of the proceeds, his wife also being aware of it, and brought a*

certain part and laid it at the apostles' feet. But Peter said, "Ananias, why has Satan filled your heart to lie to the Holy Spirit and keep back part of the price of the land for yourself? While it remained, was it not your own? And after it was sold, was it not in your own control? Why have you conceived this thing in your heart? You have not lied to men but to God."

Then Ananias, hearing these words, fell down and breathed his last. So great fear came upon all those who heard these things.

Peter spoke judgment upon them because of their decep-tion and sin. The result was that fear of the Lord came not just upon the church, but also upon the culture. Ananias and his wife Sapphira lied to the Holy Spirit. This was obviously a heinous thing to do. This should make us more aware of how we must treat the Holy Spirit. Their sin of lying to the Holy Spirit caused God to judge them. He used Peter, however, to render this judgment upon them. My reason for speaking of this is to clarify that God grants us a position as judges. Even though we might consider judg-ment "negative," the real reason for judgment is to set in place justice and divine order. God told the prophet Jere-miah that his ministry would be to destroy and then build. This statement refers to the ability to judge. Jeremiah 1:10

speaks of the authority granted Jeremiah to deal with kingdoms. God says,

> *See, I have this day set you over the nations and over*
> *the kingdoms,*
>
> *To root out and to pull down,*
>
> *To destroy and to throw down,*
>
> *To build and to plant.*

Jeremiah would be allowed to render judgments in the spirit that removed evil from nations and kingdoms. He would also be allowed to render judgments that built and established nations. Anything that happens in the natural first occurred in the spirit. When judges take their place in the spirit realm, divine order can come in the natural. As judges in the realm of the spirit, we are setting things in order in agreement with God's justice. First Corinthians 2:15 tells us those who are spiritual "judge" all things.

> *But he who is spiritual judges all things, yet he himself*
> *is rightly judged by no one.*

The words "judges" and "judged" in the Greek is "ana-krino," and it means to scrutinize, examine, and judge. It comes from the word "krino," which means to decide judicially. Clearly we see that normal believers, filled with the Spirit of God, are able to judge. Notice also that they are not "rightly judged" by anyone. In other words, people will not understand those who function in this realm of the spirit. It doesn't say they aren't judged. It says they aren't rightly judged. People who judge in the spiritual realm will be criticized and scrutinized. These believers, however, will be justified by the Lord because they are "judging" from His Spirit and heart.

This brings me to the subject we must cover. I can hear someone quoting the oft-referred-to scripture in Matthew 7:1–5, where Jesus seems to command us not to judge.

Judge not, that you be not judged. For with what judgment you judge, you will be judged; and with the measure you use, it will be measured back to you. And why do you look at the speck in your brother's eye, but do not consider the plank in your own eye? Or how can you say to your brother, "Let me remove the speck from your eye"; and look, a plank is in your own eye? Hypocrite! First remove the plank from your

own eye, and then you will see clearly to remove the
speck from your brother's eye.

This scripture is almost always cited as a declaration not to judge. We are told that judging is wrong. We are told that if we judge, we will be judged! However, if we investigate this scripture more closely, we find that is not what is being said. We are being told that if there are areas of our lives that are not in line with God and His word, we should refrain from judging. The admonition, however, is to get things right and correct so we can judge righteously. The need for righteous judgment is critical. Without righteous judgment there is NO JUSTICE. When there is NO JUSTICE, culture and society go off the rails. Ecclesiastes 8:11 shows the lack of justice produces a chaotic state in society.

Because the sentence against an evil work is not exe-
cuted speedily, therefore the heart of the sons of men is
fully set in them to do evil.

When no justice is served effectively, it eliminates a sense of fear, which typically holds people in check. The result is a society out of order and devouring itself.

I was in Singapore and was being hosted by a retired judge from the High Court, which is one step below the Supreme Court of the land. He was explaining to me the reason for the low crime rate in their society. They are a democratic society just like the United States is. However, he explained that instead of making the individual's right the ultimate goal, society as a whole was esteemed. In other words, the litmus test of their judicial system was not so much how things affected individuals as much as how they affected the society and culture as a whole. The result has been very little crime, less poverty, and a peaceful place within which to live and function. They do not deal with the sense of entitlement that plagues us Americans. The people of the culture have bred into them a sense of honor, wholesome fear, and a desire to be a productive part of culture. I am not saying that Singapore is "better" than America. I am saying, however, that when you exalt the individual above the whole, there will be a breakdown in society. Judgment that produces justice for all must involve valuing society above individual rights and privileges. This has to be taken into account in judicial activities. Decisions cannot be made just on the basis of what is good for one. They have to be made on the basis of what is good for the community and culture of which the one is a member.

When Jesus said don't judge lest you be judged, He was not saying we shouldn't judge. He was declaring that we shouldn't judge if things are not correct in our own lives. If we judge without things spiritually lined up in our lives, then we open ourselves to judgment. The truth is, if we step into a place of judgment without having been judged ourselves, we WILL be judged. The result can be devastating to us. The devil from his legal position as our adversary—"antidikos" in the Greek—will present a case against us before the Courts of Heaven. We can then find ourselves embroiled in legal issues in the spirit. This is because we have "judged" without first being "judged" or getting things set in order.

Notice in the scripture that Jesus said if we take the time and effort to get the beam or log out of our eye, "we will see" how to get the speck out of another's eye. In other words, we will be able to judge with righteous judgment and help one another. The admonition here isn't to not judge. The admonition is to judge ourselves first so we can then judge rightly. This is what the Apostle Paul said in First Corinthians 11:31–32.

> *For if we would judge ourselves, we would not be judged. But when we are judged, we are chastened*

by the Lord, that we may not be condemned with the world.

When we allow judgment into our lives through the Holy Spirit, we then become those who can render judgment. Paul further said that God judges or chastens us so we won't be condemned with the world. We will escape the consequences of sin, which the world will face. God's chastening and judging hand is actually His mercy at work. It does these two things: It causes us to escape any and all condemnation which the world will suffer, and also sets us into place so we can render judgment without the fear of being judged! This is absolutely necessary if we are to see justice enacted on earth. Again, we need natural judges but also spiritual ones so God's passion and heart can be seen in the world. The question is, will we allow the work of God to be done in us so we can take our place as "judges" in the realm of the spirit? God needs us to be positioned as judges in the Courts of Heaven. Through prayers, decrees, and declarations, we will be able to see things shift in the spirit realm so they change and line up with God's passion in the natural realm.

I would like to share three things that happened to me in regards to this concept of being a "judge" in the spirit. The first one occurred several years ago now. Mary and I were away on vacation in Hawaii. I had a very vivid dream that shook me. In my dream, an angelic being appeared to me. There was a "seat" hanging in the atmosphere that I knew I could sit in. (Sitting in a seat quite often refers to sitting in a governmental/judicial place, i.e. a throne.) I took my place in this seat. The angel then handed me a check. Instead of it being a check for money, on it was written a requirement. I understood that something was being required of me to sit in this seat. Since it was in the form of a check, God was saying, "I am giving you the grace you need to fulfill the requirement to sit in this seat." On the check was written, "No more alcohol." I know there will be those who will condemn me because I at that time drank some wine and enjoyed it. I saw nothing wrong with this and, quite honestly, still do not. I have no problem with those believers who, in moderation, partake of alcoholic beverages. This is just my personal opinion. I respect others' views, but this is mine. I knew, however, that God was saying to me, "In the place I want you to function from, you cannot partake of alcohol." Later, I would become aware that God was asking me to walk as a Nazarite in the spirit world. The Nazarite vow is found in Numbers 6:1–8 and includes three requirements. They were not allowed to drink wine, touch anything dead, nor cut their hair.

Then the LORD spoke to Moses, saying, "Speak to the children of Israel, and say to them: 'When either a man or woman consecrates an offering to take the vow of a Nazirite, to separate himself to the LORD, he shall separate himself from wine and similar drink; he shall drink neither vinegar made from wine nor vinegar made from similar drink; neither shall he drink any grape juice, nor eat fresh grapes or raisins. All the days of his separation he shall eat nothing that is produced by the grapevine, from seed to skin.

'All the days of the vow of his separation no razor shall come upon his head; until the days are fulfilled for which he separated himself to the LORD, he shall be holy. Then he shall let the locks of the hair of his head grow. All the days that he separates himself to the LORD he shall not go near a dead body. He shall not make himself unclean even for his father or his mother, for his brother or his sister, when they die, because his separation to God is on his head. All the days of his separation he shall be holy to the LORD.'"

These three things have ramifications for us in the New Testament as we consecrate our lives to the Lord. To not drink wine speaks of being under the influence of nothing but the Holy Spirit. We are to be sober and filled with the

Holy Spirit and His power. This is why the Apostle Paul wrote in Ephesians 5:18–21 that we were to be filled with the Spirit.

> *And do not be drunk with wine, in which is dissi-*
> *pation; but be filled with the Spirit, speaking to one*
> *another in psalms and hymns and spiritual songs,*
> *singing and making melody in your heart to the Lord,*
> *giving thanks always for all things to God the Father in*
> *the name of our Lord Jesus Christ, submitting to one*
> *another in the fear of God.*

We are to be under no other influence but the Spirit of the living God. When we are, we are empowered to live out the life we are made for. Another requirement of the Nazarite was to not touch a dead person or thing even if it was a close relative. The dead thing would cause defile-ment, and the consecration would be lost. This speaks of not touching "dead works." We are not to associate or be a part of anything dead. Hebrews 6:1–2 speaks of repenting of dead works.

> *Therefore, leaving the discussion of the elementary*
> *principles of Christ, let us go on to perfection, not*
> *laying again the foundation of repentance from dead*

*works and of faith toward God, of the doctrine of
baptisms, of laying on of hands, of resurrection of the
dead, and of eternal judgment.*

Dead works is one of the things we are to repent of and
move away from. This can be moral and/or ethical issues.
I also believe it can speak of dead religious activities that
have no life in them. There are definitely dead religious
practices that are lifeless and useless in the spirit world. We
are to repent of these. Paul spoke of these to Timothy in
Second Timothy 3:5. Paul warns him of people,

*Having a form of godliness but denying its power. And
from such people turn away!*

Notice that Timothy is exhorted to turn away from these
people. Timothy was not to allow into his life those who
looked godly but actually had no power to influence him.
He wasn't to touch anything that was dead. Traditions,
legalisms, and activities void of the life of God were to be
avoided. In the New Testament, the vow of the Nazarite
isn't about not going to funerals and not being involved
with dead corpses. It is about not being influenced by those
who have no real spiritual life in them even though they
are still naturally breathing. We are not to defile ourselves

with dead religion. This would include rituals and traditions with no real spiritual value. They may soothe the
conscience but produce no real change or godliness. The
third requirement of a Nazarite was to never cut their hair.
My understanding was they could trim their hair to make
it manageable but not cut it. This was an outward sign of
their inward consecration. Hair speaks of glory and mod-
est covering (see 1 Corinthians 11:15). Of course, we are
familiar with Samson's hair, which represented his strength
and anointing and consecration by God. Samson was a
Nazarite from his birth, as were Samuel and John the Baptist. All three of them functioned as God's judges on earth.
Their Nazarite vow was what allowed them their judgeship
in the spirit dimension. It was their consecration by God
that granted them their place of authority.

In addition to the "no alcohol" requirement, I also had
a dream where my hair was down to my waist. I knew God
was telling me that I had a position in the spirit realm as a
Nazarite with judge's privileges and responsibilities.

Let me tell you the third and final account. I was in
Switzerland teaching on the Courts of Heaven. I was lead-
ing the group through an activity of looking into the spirit
to see what they were wearing. We all have clothing on in
the spirit that speaks of our place, authority, function, and

standing there. Remember that the priests in the Old Testament had to wear certain garments and garb to function as a priest. This is seen in Exodus 28:2–4.

> *And you shall make holy garments for Aaron your brother, for glory and for beauty. So you shall speak to all who are gifted artisans, whom I have filled with the spirit of wisdom, that they may make Aaron's garments, to consecrate him, that he may minister to Me as priest. And these are the garments which they shall make: a breastplate, an ephod, a robe, a skillfully woven tunic, a turban, and a sash. So they shall make holy garments for Aaron your brother and his sons, that he may minister to Me as priest.*

These garments caused Aaron to be recognized in the spiritual realm and granted him a role. As New Testament believers, we, too, are "kings and priests" to our God. We also have garments we have been granted to wear in the spirit realm. These garments give us a place of authority and activity in that dimension. This is why Joshua, a high priest, was given new, fresh garments to wear in Zechariah 3:3–7. It allowed him to function in the realm of the spirit.

Now Joshua was clothed with filthy garments, and was standing before the Angel.

Then He answered and spoke to those who stood before Him, saying, "Take away the filthy garments from him." And to him He said, "See, I have removed your iniquity from you, and I will clothe you with rich robes."

And I said, "Let them put a clean turban on his head."

So they put a clean turban on his head, and they put the clothes on him. And the Angel of the LORD stood by.

Then the Angel of the LORD admonished Joshua, saying, "Thus says the LORD of hosts:

'If you will walk in My ways,
And if you will keep My command,
Then you shall also judge My house,
And likewise have charge of My courts;
I will give you places to walk
Among these who stand here.'"

Notice that when this priest was given fresh, clean clothes to wear, it resulted in him "walking among these who stand here." This was in the spirit dimension. His clothes granted him a functional place in a judicial realm of the spirit. The priest had judicial responsibilities. For instance, when someone had leprosy, only the priest could proclaim them clean so they could return to society. In Leviticus 13:2–3, God makes a decree that priests should examine and make a judgment regarding leprosy.

> *When a man has on the skin of his body a swelling,*
> *a scab, or a bright spot, and it becomes on the skin of*
> *his body like a leprous sore, then he shall be brought to*
> *Aaron the priest or to one of his sons the priests. The*
> *priest shall examine the sore on the skin of the body;*
> *and if the hair on the sore has turned white, and the*
> *sore appears to be deeper than the skin of his body, it is*
> *a leprous sore. Then the priest shall examine him, and*
> *pronounce him unclean.*

If someone was proclaimed unclean as a result of leprosy, they were ostracized from society. They were not allowed around anyone. They had to proclaim, "Unclean, Unclean," if anyone came near them. It was the priest's job to render this judgment and decision. Also, if someone was cleansed of leprosy, only the priest could verify this change. In Leviticus 14:2, God claims that it is the priest who has the power to proclaim a leper cleansed from his leprosy.

> *This shall be the law of the leper for the day of his cleansing: He shall be brought to the priest.*

The priest had the responsibility of judgment over those with leprosy and in other situations. Being a priest carries responsibility for judgment. For this role in the spirit, we need to put on the right clothes.

Now, back to my encounter in Switzerland. I was not "trying" to see anything concerning myself as I led this group through this activation. I was simply trying to help those to whom I was ministering see themselves in the spirit. Suddenly, I saw myself standing in the spirit realm in black judge's robes. I was somewhat taken back. I didn't yet understand the concept that we could occupy the position of a judge in the spirit dimension. The man who was translating for me, who is very prophetic, then began to laugh. I had not mentioned what I saw. I was still processing it. He suddenly says, "I see an angel here, and every time you say something, he is recording it in writing." I knew this was because of my position as a judge. My words had power and authority in this dimension because of the seat I sat in and what I was wearing in this spirit realm.

Since that time, I have come to realize I have some authority as a judge in the spirit dimension. I try to measure my words because of this authority. I also recognize that I can make decrees because of the position I have been granted. The truth, however, is so can you. Again, the Apostle Paul writing to the Corinthian church said those who are spiritual can judge (see 1 Corinthians 2:15). There is a place in the Courts of Heaven that we are to operate from. From this place in the Courts of Heaven, we can issue judgments, decrees, and decisions. Heaven needs God's people to take their place as judges in the realms of the spirit. When we occupy these places, our words of decree and declaration can cause things to shift. Things will move in the invisible realm so that which is visible can line up with godly order. We can do this from the Courts of Heaven as those who have been granted the right to judge!

Here is a decree, declaration, and petition you can give to the Lord and His Courts to help you move into this position as a judge.

I come before You, Lord, who is the Judge of all the earth. As I stand before Your Courts, I request the right to take my place as a judge in Your Courts. I desire, Lord, to be able to release judgments that will set in order Your kingdom's will on the earth. I desire your passion for justice to be seen on the earth. You, Lord, are just in Your nature and person. The justness of who You are is the source of our patience. Your Word declares in Revelation 13:10,

> *He who leads into captivity shall go into captivity; he who kills with the sword must be killed with the sword. Here is the patience and the faith of the saints.*

I thank You, Lord, for Your justice. I wait for Your justice to be manifested on the earth. This is my patience and faith as one who belongs to You. Thank You so much.

As I take my place as a judge, I allow the Holy Spirit to "judge" me and chasten me according to Your Word. I invite and yield myself to the searching of the Spirit. I welcome the Holy Spirit's work to reveal and take out of my life any "log" or "beam" that would not allow me to see clearly as a judge.

I ask that any wrong perspective, any wrong idea or concept, or any wrong motive be removed from me. I want to give only righteous judgments before You.

As a judge in the spirit realm before You, I ask that I might take my seat. The place You have ordained for me to occupy, I by faith take that place. I ask that any mantle and anointing associated with this seat now come upon me. I ask that I might function in the fear of the Lord as a judge in the realm of the spirit. Thanks so much, Lord, for allowing me to make decrees, issue declarations, release prayers, and present petitions before You. I ask, Lord, that things would come to divine order in the natural as things shift in the spirit with these decrees. Lord, may breakthroughs come because of You allowing me to function as a judge from the Courts of Heaven. Thank You so much for this honor and privilege. In Jesus's name, so be it!

CHAPTER 5

OPENING THE
COURTS OF HEAVEN

AS I have been aware of the Courts of Heaven for many years now, I have learned it can be helpful to ask for the Courts to be open. Let me explain. I believe that when Jesus died that His blood and all He did grants us access to heavenly dimensions. This is why Paul spoke in Ephesians 2:6 of being seated in heavenly places. He says that God made us alive in Jesus,

> *And raised us up together, and made us sit together in the heavenly places in Christ Jesus.*

We have been positioned by virtue of Jesus's work on our behalf. However, we must access this place by faith.

Romans 5:2 makes an intriguing statement. It says we are at peace with God through Jesus,

> *through whom also we have access by faith into this grace in which we stand, and rejoice in hope of the glory of God.*

Notice that we are "standing" in a place we have to "access" by faith. Getting the benefits of what Jesus made available to us requires faith. So even though we are standing in a certain dimension, we have to access it by faith. This is why asking the Courts to open for us and allow us entrance requires activation. Through this activity, we are using our faith to access where we already stand. That is a biblical concept.

A further reason for seeking to have the Courts open to us is because we are approaching God as Judge. Hebrews 12:23 clearly says we have come,

> *To the general assembly and church of the firstborn who are registered in heaven, to God the Judge of all, to the spirits of just men made perfect.*

In these verses, God is not revealed as Father or even Lord, King, or Savior. He is revealed as Judge. In the natural, when you come before a judge, it can be a terrifying thing. The words of the judge have the power to set the course of your life for great amounts of time to come. Usually, judges who rule courts in the natural realm require honor and appropriate behavior while you are in their court. The court and the judge who rules the court are to be respected. How much more the Judge of all the earth! His Courts and His Judgeship are to be honored. This is why when we approach God as Judge, we should operate according to certain protocols. There should be reverential fear before this Judge. This is what the early church walked in. Acts 9:31 declares this was a part of the life of the church.

> *Then the churches throughout all Judea, Galilee, and Samaria had peace and were edified. And walking in the fear of the Lord and in the comfort of the Holy Spirit, they were multiplied.*

Coming before the Judge of all the earth should require fear of the Lord. Even the Apostle Paul spoke of the "terror" of the Lord. Second Corinthians 5:10–11 shows Paul being motivated out of what he calls "the terror of the Lord."

> *For we must all appear before the judgment seat of Christ, that each one may receive the things done in the body, according to what he has done, whether good or bad. Knowing, therefore, the terror of the Lord, we persuade men; but we are well known to God, and I also trust are well known in your consciences.*

Paul said he was acquainted with the terror of the Lord. This caused him to seek to persuade others. He was afraid for them in the final judgment. The final judgment will be the most monumental time in the Courts of Heaven. We will stand to give account of our life and deeds before the Lord. I believe it is appropriate to consider and examine ourselves from time to time in light of this reality.

I do not want to leave the impression that we should be tormented by fear. This is not the fear of the Lord. It is, however, a sobering realization that He is God and we are to obey Him. It is an awareness that if I obey, blessings will come, but if I disobey, heartache can be the result. The fear of the Lord presses me to live within the boundaries the Lord has for my life. My point is we need to be possessed by a healthy fear of the Lord. We need to be aware of who our God is. Not only is He our Father, Friend, Lord, King, and Shepherd. He is also the Judge. When we come to stand before Him as Judge, all things are made open and manifest. Hebrews 4:13 declares that God is aware of everything.

> *And there is no creature hidden from His sight, but all things are naked and open to the eyes of Him to whom we must give account.*

When it says, "we must give account," it is speaking of the Lord as Judge. As we approach the Lord's Courts, we must make ourselves available for Him to examine. This is why when I approach the Courts of Heaven, I almost always present myself as a living sacrifice to the Lord. This is found in Romans 12:1.

> *I beseech you therefore, brethren, by the mercies of God, that you present your bodies a living sacrifice, holy, acceptable to God, which is your reasonable service.*

I come before Him with fear and ask to be accepted by Him. I then ask for the blood of Jesus to speak on my behalf and allow me the right to stand in His Courts. Hebrews 12:24 declares that the blood of Jesus is speaking for me before the Lord. It says that we come,

> *To Jesus the Mediator of the new covenant, and to the*
> *blood of sprinkling that speaks better things than that*
> *of Abel.*

The blood of Jesus is speaking for me and granting me the right to be accepted before the Lord. I, however, am allowing the Lord to examine my life. This is because the blood keeps on cleansing every sin according to First John 1:7.

> *But if we walk in the light as He is in the light, we*
> *have fellowship with one another, and the blood of*
> *Jesus Christ His Son cleanses us from all sin.*

The tense of the word "cleanses" in the Greek is to say "it keeps on cleansing" us from all sin. So when we come before the Lord in the light, or the place of examination and exposure, the blood keeps perfecting and cleansing us. As I stand before the Lord in surrender and submission, I allow the searching of His light to permeate me and expose dark places in me. I can then repent and allow the blood of His Son to cleanse me of all defilements. This is always the first thing that we do as we approach the Courts of Heaven and ask them to open. We then by faith take our place among the other heavenly beings that exist there, including Jesus, our advocate. First John 2:1 makes the powerful reference to Jesus legally representing us to the Father in His Court.

> *My little children, these things I write to you, so that you may not sin. And if anyone sins, we have an Advocate with the Father, Jesus Christ the righteous.*

The word "Advocate" is the Greek word "parakletos," and it means a legal aid, an intercessor, or one who stands on our behalf. Jesus can show up in these Court settings to give necessary testimony concerning us.

Other heavenly beings can also come into this setting: angels with different functions, people from the Cloud of Witnesses, different realms of heaven, books that contain necessary information, and demonic powers to present cases against us. These can be present in the Courts of Heaven as we enter and begin to operate here. The first priority, however, is to see the Courts open and step into them.

Here is a prayer to help us see this dimension open and gain access to that which we stand.

Lord, I thank You for all Jesus has done for me. I thank You that I have been repositioned in the realms of the spirit because of Jesus's work on the cross. As I now stand in these dimensions, I by faith ask access to Your Courts. I ask that the doors of the Courts be open for me and that I be granted the right to stand in Your Holy Place. (At this point, visualize in your spirit standing before these doors. Different people see different things, but just begin to "look" here.) Hebrews 5:14 says we begin to learn our spiritual senses by using them.

> *But solid food belongs to those who are of full age, that is, those who by reason of use have their senses exercised to discern both good and evil.*

(Begin to exercise your "seeing sense." Don't be afraid to "look" and see what you are seeing.)

(As the doors open, "step" across the threshold into the Courts. "Look" into the spirit and see what you see. I usually am aware of the Cloud of Witnesses in a balcony type setting. I also see God the Judge. His seat is very high, and I normally can't see His head or face. You may see Jesus. You also may see angels in the Courts. Sometimes, there is an angel keeping record of all that is happening.)

Lord, as I stand before Your Courts, I present myself as a living sacrifice before You according to Romans 12:1. I ask You to examine me and purify me by Your blood of any and all defilements. Lord, I want to be holy as I stand here in Your presence. Please forgive me of every sin, trespass, and iniquity. I ask that Your blood would speak for me as I stand here before You.

(Be aware of any words being spoken against you by a demonic force. Should you hear, see, feel, or discern anything being brought against you, begin to repent of it. Ask for the blood of Jesus to speak on your behalf.)

Lord, I acknowledge that which is being spoken against me. I acknowledge these accusations, and I repent for any and all of them. I ask for Your blood to speak for me. I am sorry for that of which I am guilty. Would you forgive me and revoke the rights of these who speak against me. Would You by Your blood stand on my behalf and silence every accusation against me. I am sorry for my sin. Thank You, Lord Jesus, for all that You have done and do for me. Let, I pray, this case against me be dismissed and removed.

> (At this point, the Court may allow you to make a request. If so, begin to present your petition before the Court, listening and being sensitive to anything going on in this sphere.)

> (As you get ready to leave the Court, do not just end it. Be careful to thank the Lord for allowing you time there and also to seal by the blood of Jesus anything that was done.)

Lord, thank You so much for allowing me to tread Your Courts. I honor and bless You. I ask that the work done in me would be established. I ask that it be sealed by the blood of Jesus and the power of the Holy Spirit. Thank you so much for allowing me to encounter You and the Courts of Heaven. In Jesus's name. Amen!

CHAPTER 6

CLEANSING BLOODLINE ISSUES

O NE of the things the devil uses against us the most is the iniquity in our bloodline. Most of us are aware of our own sins and transgressions. We know our own stuff. We recognize where we have fallen short. However, things buried in our bloodlines can be a little more difficult to deal with. Remember that when Daniel and others were seeking to get Israel out of captivity and back to their inheritance, they repented for their personal sins and the iniquity of their fathers. Daniel 9:16–17 shows some of this repentance.

O Lord, according to all Your righteousness, I pray, let Your anger and Your fury be turned away from Your

> *city Jerusalem, Your holy mountain; because for our*
> *sins, and for the iniquities of our fathers, Jerusalem*
> *and Your people are a reproach to all those around*
> *us. Now therefore, our God, hear the prayer of Your*
> *servant, and his supplications, and for the Lord's sake*
> *cause Your face to shine on Your sanctuary, which is*
> *desolate.*

Notice that Daniel made his supplication and intercession concerning their sins and iniquities for the Lord's sake. In other words, he was pointing out to God His interest in this matter. God, as a covenant-keeping God, would want to see His people restored to their land and inheritance. He would desire His purposes in them fulfilled but also His reputation in them maintained.

When Daniel repented for the iniquities of the fathers, he was not seeking to change their eternal destiny. The Bible says it is appointed to man once to die and then to face the judgment. We find this in Hebrews 9:27.

> *And as it is appointed for men to die once, but after*
> *this the judgment.*

Every man will be recompensed for the life he has lived. Nothing can change this. However, repenting for the iniquity of the fathers removes satan's legal right to use it against us. We are not seeking to change eternal destinies. When we take responsibility for our own sins and the sins of our bloodline, we are dealing with the legal issues satan would use to build a case against us. We see this in the life of Israel as a nation. In Second Samuel 21:1, we see David discerning why there was a drought and famine in Israel for three years.

> *Now there was a famine in the days of David for three years, year after year; and David inquired of the LORD. And the LORD answered, "It is because of Saul and his bloodthirsty house, because he killed the Gibeonites."*

Saul had killed the Gibeonites with whom Joshua had made a covenant. You'll remember that Joshua had not inquired of the Lord what to do about the Gibeonites when he encountered them. They made up a story that they were from a far-off land and had come to worship the God of Joshua and the Israelites. In reality, they were a people living in the Promised Land who Joshua was supposed to destroy. They deceived Joshua, and Joshua entered into a covenant with them. Even though the covenant was made in deception, it still stood before heaven. Joshua and the leaders gave their word. You can find this story in Joshua 9:1–15. Now, Saul has broken the covenant with the Gibeonites. This broken covenant had granted the devil the legal right to shut up the heavens and stop the rain. Saul had done this 70 years before the famine occurred. Now, all these years later, there's a famine because of a broken covenant from 70 years prior. David and all the people had been praying for three years for rain, yet none had come. When David understands why the famine has happened, he sets the covenant with the Gibeonites back in place. The Bible then makes an astounding statement in Second Samuel 21:14.

> *They buried the bones of Saul and Jonathan his son in the country of Benjamin in Zelah, in the tomb of Kish his father. So they performed all that the king commanded. And after that God heeded the prayer for the land.*

God heeded the prayer for the land. The same prayer that had been prayed for three years was suddenly answered. The difference was the legal right in the history of Israel to resist rain was revoked through broken covenants! God could now answer the prayer of His people because the legal right in the spirit realm granting the devil power through a broken and dishonored covenant was now removed. If we are to see breakthrough, many times we must deal with the history of sin or iniquity in our bloodlines. The devil uses them as a legal right to reduce us to less than what God desires.

To discern iniquity in the bloodline, we should understand the nature of iniquity. The word "iniquity" in the Hebrew is the word "avon," and it means something perverted. It means to be twisted. So iniquity in the bloodline twists the desires and purposes of God. It twists the moral compass of a person's life. It twists desires from that which is good to that which is evil. Iniquity isn't just about a single sin. Iniquity is about the twisting of nature. This is why when we are born again, we receive a new nature. Second Peter 1:4 tells us we have received the divine nature, or the nature of God Himself. It is God's excellence and glory,

> By which have been given to us exceedingly great
> and precious promises, that through these you may
> be partakers of the divine nature, having escaped the
> corruption that is in the world through lust.

Through the divine nature, we escape the corruption that is in the world. Yet that which we receive at salvation has to dominate and empower us. Even though we have the nature of God in us, the issues in our bloodline will try to work against us. Notice that the Apostle Paul in speaking to Titus gave him instructions about ministering in the Cretan culture. Titus 1:10–13 shows us a perversion in a bloodline that has affected a culture.

> *For there are many insubordinate, both idle talkers and deceivers, especially those of the circumcision, whose mouths must be stopped, who subvert whole households, teaching things which they ought not, for the sake of dishonest gain. One of them, a prophet of their own, said, "Cretans are always liars, evil beasts, lazy gluttons." This testimony is true. Therefore rebuke them sharply, that they may be sound in the faith.*

Paul realized that even though these people were saved and born again, issues in their bloodline were still affecting them. Their culture had been twisted to be liars, evil beasts, and gluttons. Paul's commandment to Titus was to rebuke them and challenge them to let the new nature in them arise. They could not conform to that which had fashioned their culture for generations. They had to deal with their bloodline issues so it didn't continue to twist them and pervert who they were meant to be.

In dealing with bloodline issues, we should be aware of anything that twists the real intent of God for our family. For instance, the Cretans were not meant to be liars, evil beasts, and gluttons. Generations of iniquity had fashioned them into this. Perhaps there are addiction issues in your bloodline. Maybe there are sexual issues there. Perhaps anger issues are present. Maybe there is violence. It could be anything. I challenge people to look at themselves and their siblings, their parents, and their own children. Within these three generations, you will see bloodline issues. Begin to repent of these things. As you exhaust these, then ask the Lord for any further revelation you might need. If there are no more realizations, then be at peace. You can only deal with the knowledge you have. I tell folks that when you have dealt with everything you know, then use Colossians 2:14. It says that God made us alive with Jesus,

> *Having wiped out the handwriting of requirements that was against us, which was contrary to us. And He has taken it out of the way, having nailed it to the cross.*

The "handwriting of ordinance" refers to that which the devil is using to build a case against us. After I have prayed over everything I know and discern, I ask that Colossians 2:14 be applied to my life. I ask that every case against me, known or unknown, be dismissed, based on what Jesus did for me on the cross. I have seen great results simply taking this by faith and executing it.

Here is a prayer that can be prayed to come before the Courts of Heaven and cleanse our bloodlines.

Lord, as I come into Your Courts, I stand before You. Lord, I thank You that what Jesus did for me on the cross now speaks on my behalf before Your Courts. I repent for my own personal sins and transgressions, but I also bring the iniquity of my bloodline to You. I ask that anything the devil would legally accuse me of would now be revealed.

I bring my bloodline to You through my father (name your father) and through my mother (name your mother) all the way back to Adam and Eve. I ask that anything that the devil would legally be bringing against me would be known.

I repent of all iniquities I have discerned naturally. (Deal with each issue separately. Go through them one by one, repenting of that which has twisted the bloodline and generations.) I now ask for the blood of Jesus to speak for me and my bloodline. I ask that any and every legal right of the devil to use these things would now be revoked. Thank You, Lord Jesus, so much for Your blood that speaks for me.

I repent for any and all iniquities I discern in my bloodline through my father and my mother prophetically. I ask that anything that needs to be exposed in my bloodline would now be seen. Anything the devil, as my legal opponent, would bring against me, I ask that he be made to show it. (Be sensitive at this stage to anything you see, hear, or feel. Anything that is discerned, whether you know about it naturally or not, repent of it.)

I also, Lord, thank You for Colossians 2:14 that declares You took away every case against me on the cross. I ask, Lord, that anything known or unknown would be removed. I ask that the right of the devil to legally use this against me is now revoked. Thank you so much for nailing all these things against me to Your cross. I receive it and accept it in Jesus's name. Amen.

CHAPTER 7

OUR BOOK OF DESTINY

FOR anyone who has followed the teaching on the Courts of Heaven, you will recognize the importance of "Books of Destiny" in the Courts. There are actual books/scrolls in heaven that declare our purpose for existence on the earth. Psalm 139:16 reveals David's understanding of this.

> *Your eyes saw my substance, being yet unformed.*
> *And in Your book they all were written,*
> *The days fashioned for me,*
> *When as yet there were none of them.*

David is declaring that there is a book in heaven that speaks not only of his makeup but also of his destiny and purpose in life. This is quite an interesting scripture. Before a book existed, God *saw* our substance. Our books had their beginning through God *seeing* something before it existed that was yet unformed. Our destiny and purpose began through the prophetic nature of God as a seer. As I shared briefly in a previous chapter, God saw us functioning in the earth realm before it was naturally there. He then wrote in a book two things connected to our function. He first wrote my substance. I believe this has to do with our DNA, what makes us unique and who we are as individuals. It has to do with our desires and what we gravitate to. It has to do with our gifts and abilities. It has to do with what we are good at and what we are not good at. All these things coincide with the destiny and purpose we were made for. So one of the best ways to discern what is in your book is to look at your desires. Also, you should look at the gifts and abilities you have. They will be clues to what you were made for. These things are different for each individual. God saw these gifts and put them down in a book that then predestined us. Some people get all crazy about predestination. It simply means God has a thought-out plan for our life. We do not have to agree with that plan. Yet we are the most satisfied when our might and efforts line up with His plan for us. Ephesians 1:11 tells us we have an inheritance connected to our predestined state.

In Him also we have obtained an inheritance, being predestined according to the purpose of Him who works all things according to the counsel of His will.

What is written in our books is according to His purpose. This means that God cannot get His purpose done on earth without His people reaching their destinies. This is the reason why the devil fights against us, so he might apprehend our destinies. We also see Ephesians 2:10 telling us about God's thought-out plan.

For we are His workmanship, created in Christ Jesus for good works, which God prepared beforehand that we should walk in them.

Notice there are things we are to walk in that were prepared beforehand. This refers to our book/scroll of destiny in heaven. When we are called His workmanship, this is the Greek term "poiema," and it means something that is made. It also can refer to a work of art. The Greek word itself is the word from which we get *poem* in our English language. God works in us to fashion our desires to reflect what is written in our books/scrolls. A poem has to be read in rhythm to get the full effect. When we step into our destiny, we will discover a rhythm of the Spirit we sync into.

Matthew 11:28–30 (from the Message translation) makes some significant statements about discovering this rhythm.

> *Are you tired? Worn out? Burned out on religion? Come to me. Get away with me and you'll recover your life. I'll show you how to take a real rest. Walk with me and work with me—watch how I do it. Learn the unforced rhythms of grace. I won't lay anything heavy or ill-fitting on you. Keep company with me and you'll learn to live freely and lightly.*

Discovering the unforced rhythms of grace awakens us to being His workmanship. We begin to realize how we were made and what we were made for. The strife and frustration of life can cease. We begin to get into the rhythm of our destiny. I remember several years ago of prophesying that God wanted to "take us out of the grind of life and put us into the groove." What I understood was that so many live in a striving posture. They are just "grinding" it out. God, however, wants us to live in His "groove" or niche. He desires us to be in a place where life is easy and our burden is light. Even as I write this, I can sense the longing of the Lord to bring us into this place we were made for and He saw for us before time began.

The second thing written in our book of destiny is the span of our life and what we are to accomplish. We are told the *days were fashioned for us before there was any of them*. Again as I stated earlier, I think it's interesting that it doesn't say weeks, months, or years. It says *days*, or the details and specifics of our lives. God is not just in charge of the big picture, but is also helping us in our daily lives to fulfill what is written in our books. Every day we should surrender our lives to His purposes. There may be a *day* that shifts us into a part of our destiny that if missed, can be catastrophic. I believe this is why the psalmist in Psalm 118:22–24 spoke of the day the Lord had made.

> *The stone which the builders rejected*
> *Has become the chief cornerstone.*
> *This was the LORD's doing;*
> *It is marvelous in our eyes.*
> *This is the day the LORD has made;*
> *We will rejoice and be glad in it.*

The day when Jesus, the rejected One, was declared and set as the chief cornerstone was the *day the Lord had made*. In other words, it was an appointed time for this to happen. That day changed the future of the earth and all its inhabitants. God also has days He has made for you. These days are strategic times when you shift into all that was written in your book. These days cannot be missed. They are the "kairos" moments of God. Luke 19:43–44 shows Jesus telling the nation of Israel what was going to happen because they missed this "kairos" time.

> *For days will come upon you when your enemies will build an embankment around you, surround you and close you in on every side, and level you, and your children within you, to the ground; and they will not leave in you one stone upon another, because you did not know the time of your visitation.*

The word "time" is the Greek word "kairos," and it means an occasion, a set or proper time. We normally think of a "kairos" moment as a time that God has ordained. In this time, you experience breakthrough or the future you were meant for. The nation of Israel, by not recognizing Jesus as Messiah, missed their time of visitation. The result was a future God never intended for them. Because they did not believe the revelation of who Jesus is, they lost what God intended for them. Jesus wept over them because of this. We, too, can miss that for which we were made and what is written in our books if we don't embrace the day that was fashioned for us before time began. May we be sensitive to the Holy Spirit so we never fall into this trap.

Also the *days being fashioned for us* speaks of the length of our time on the earth. It also speaks of the purpose and destiny connected to those days. God has ordained the length of our life so we can fulfill all that is written in our book. It is our job to discover what is in our book and to fulfill it. I believe we will be judged, when we stand before the Lord, by how much of our book we fulfilled. The Bible teaches that we will each stand before the judgment seat of Christ and give an account of our lives (see 2 Corinthians 5:10). This judgment will be based not on whether we did good things but on whether we did the "God" thing for our lives. Did we fulfill what was assigned to us in our book? First Corinthians 3:11–15 speaks of the day of judgment.

> *For no other foundation can anyone lay than that which is laid, which is Jesus Christ. Now if anyone builds on this foundation with gold, silver, precious stones, wood, hay, straw, each one's work will become clear; for the Day will declare it, because it will be revealed by fire; and the fire will test each one's work, of what sort it is. If anyone's work which he has built on it endures, he will receive a reward. If anyone's*

*work is burned, he will suffer loss; but he himself will
be saved, yet so as through fire.*

We must make sure that our works are gold, silver, and
precious stone so they are preserved in the fire of His judgment. Wood, hay, and straw are not necessarily "evil" works.
They can be good things but were not what is written in our
book. The Lord will reward only what was written in our
book. May we discover all that is in our book and begin
to live it out with a passion. I want my life to count for
the kingdom of God and to be a part of seeing His purpose
fulfilled on the earth.

Daniel 7:10 shows us the connection between the Books
of Destiny in heaven and the Courts of Heaven.

*A fiery stream issued
And came forth from before Him.
A thousand thousands ministered to Him;
Ten thousand times ten thousand stood before Him.
The court was seated,
And the books were opened.*

Notice that the Court was seated and the books were
open. The reason for this is twofold. First, the cases that

are going to be presented are going to come from the books. Second, it will take the courtroom's operation to get what is in the books released fully on the earth. This is because satan uses legal things to stop us from getting all that is meant for us. We must know how to present our case in the Courts from the Books of Destiny in heaven. We must learn how to fight for what we were made for in the Courts! This occurred with Peter in the Scriptures. In Luke 22:31–32, we see the devil's strategies to stop Peter's influence.

> *And the Lord said, "Simon, Simon! Indeed, Satan has asked for you, that he may sift you as wheat. But I have prayed for you, that your faith should not fail; and when you have returned to Me, strengthen your brethren."*

The word "asked" is the Greek word "exaiteomai," and it means to demand for trial. Satan had an understanding of the purpose of God written in Peter's book. He knew if this weren't disrupted, Peter would impact the world with the powers of the kingdom of God. His strategy to hinder this was to take Peter to trial. Satan demanded a date in the Courts to accuse Peter and bring the case he had against Peter. He was seeking a legal right to devour Peter and what was written in his book. We know that Jesus stood on behalf of Peter and secured the destiny heaven had pre-scribed for Peter.

Lest we dismiss our responsibility to do the same for others and ourselves, we should realize Jesus did this as man and not as God. When Jesus walked the earth, He never did anything as God but only as a man *filled with God*. Philippians 2:5–8 tells us that Jesus did not touch His divine abilities while living on the earth even though He was God. He lived totally as a man.

> *Let this mind be in you which was also in Christ*
> *Jesus, who, being in the form of God, did not consider*
> *it robbery to be equal with God, but made Himself*
> *of no reputation, taking the form of a bondservant,*
> *and coming in the likeness of men. And being found*
> *in appearance as a man, He humbled Himself and*
> *became obedient to the point of death, even the death*
> *of the cross.*

Jesus had to live fully as a man to redeem us. A man, Adam, had lost creation, and a man, Jesus, had to win it back. If Jesus ever touched His Godhood during His time on the earth, His right to be the Savior would have been forfeited. So again, He never did anything as God, but relegated Himself to function as a human, as we must. He lived totally as a man filled with God through the Holy Spirit. So when He prayed for Peter in the Courts of Heaven, He did this as a man. This means we, too, as human beings have access to the Courts to perceive what is in our books of destiny and to secure that destiny as well.

Here is a prayer we can pray to begin to apprehend that which was foreordained for us before time began.

Lord, as I come to stand before Your Courts, I thank You that I have a book in heaven. Thank You so much that You thought of me before time began and wrote my destiny and purpose in a book in heaven. As I stand before You, I declare in Your Courts, "I want all that is in my book. I want to fulfill my destiny that is connected to Your purposes on the earth." Lord, that which you saw concerning me before time began, I ask that this might be "my life." I choose that which you have chosen for me.

As I stand before Your Courts, Lord, I lay down my life. As best I can, through the power of Your Spirit according to Romans 12:1, I present myself as a living sacrifice, holy and acceptable to you. I ask also that according to Ephesians 4:1, I might have a walk worthy of the calling that was determined for me, written in the book in heaven.

I also ask, Lord, that any case or accusation the devil would have against me before Your Courts would be silenced by the blood of Jesus. Lord, I thank You that Your blood speaks for me, and I agree with its testimony according to Hebrews 12:24. Lord, I thank You that Your blood grants God the legal right to forgive me, remember me, and redeem me to the purpose that is in my book. Just as Peter's destiny and purpose was secured from the Courts of Heaven, so, Lord, I thank You that my destiny is secured as well. Lord, I declare before Your Courts that I am Your servant, so please use me. I ask that my life might count for the kingdom of God as it is recorded in the books of destiny in heaven.

Lord, I also ask that according to Ephesians 2:10, I might walk and live as Your workmanship. I realize, Lord, that Your grace makes me Your work of art and a display of Your splendor and glory. I ask before Your Courts that I would live in the rhythms of Your grace. I ask, Lord, that You would take me "out of the grind of life, and put me into Your groove." Lord, would You now bring about my empowerment through Your Spirit that from Your strength, I could fulfill all that is written in the books of destiny for me. Lord, I desire with great passion to fulfill Your will. Please accept my request before You and let all that would resist my petition be revoked. Thank You, Lord, so much for loving me. I look forward with expectation to fulfilling all that is in my book in heaven. In Jesus's name, Amen!

CHAPTER 8

POSSESSING YOUR BOOK

We should be aware as we seek to secure our destiny that it is not something we create—it is something we discover. According to Second Timothy 1:9, Paul told Timothy that purpose and grace were allotted to them before time began. He says that it is God,

Who has saved us and called us with a holy calling,
not according to our works, but according to His own
purpose and grace which was given to us in Christ
Jesus before time began.

This is an amazing statement. Before there was the sun, moon, or stars, all of which marked time, God apportioned to each of us purpose and grace. Purpose is what is written in our book, and grace is the power to fulfill it. So all of this has been waiting on us to discover it and step into it. One of the problems is that it is possible to NOT possess your book in the spirit realm. Even though it has been written and exists there, we might not have it. The reason we might not possess it in the spirit realm is the demonic has taken it captive because of issues in our bloodline or generational history. In other words, somewhere in our ancestral line someone sold us to demonic powers. This has nothing to do with us going to heaven when we die. It does, however, have a great impact on whether we see heaven come to earth in the here and now and whether we fulfill our destiny! The accuser would use this as a legal right to keep us out of all that was written in our book. Remember that his motivation is not to stop our happiness, but to frustrate the purposes of God on the earth. Could this have been some of what the legal case was against Peter that Jesus had to undo before the Courts of Heaven? I'm sure it played in somewhere. All of us have issues in our bloodline that can be used against us legally to thwart the fulfillment of our destiny and purpose. Remember that fixing bloodline issues can be critical to removing and revoking any and every legal case the devil would use against us. Without undoing legal issues in our history, we can feel like we have a bungee cord tied to our back. No matter how hard we seem to struggle, we can never get into the destiny God made us for. We seem to be pulling against something that will not let us go. This problem can come from bloodline issues.

In regards to our book and the devil's attempts to take it captive, I always think about Esau. Esau, by birthright, should have been the one to carry the promise God made to Abraham and Isaac. However, because he despised his birthright and sold it to Jacob, what should have been his was lost. Genesis 25:30–34 shows Esau making this transaction with Jacob. Esau actually traded away his birthright for a bowl of stew.

> And Esau said to Jacob, "Please feed me with that same red stew, for I am weary." Therefore his name was called Edom.
>
> But Jacob said, "Sell me your birthright as of this day."
>
> And Esau said, "Look, I am about to die; so what is this birthright to me?"
>
> Then Jacob said, "Swear to me as of this day."
>
> So he swore to him, and sold his birthright to Jacob. And Jacob gave Esau bread and stew of lentils; then

> *he ate and drank, arose, and went his way. Thus*
> *Esau despised his birthright.*

As bad as it was for Esau to trade away his birthright, he also traded away the destiny of his family and a whole nation. For instance, they were ruled over by the descendants of Jacob. David was descended from Jacob. We see this as history progressed. Just a couple of scriptures highlight this. Second Samuel 8:14 shows how David exercised power over them.

> *He also put garrisons in Edom; throughout all Edom*
> *he put garrisons, and all the Edomites became David's*
> *servants. And the* LORD *preserved David wherever he*
> *went.*

The Edomites, who are the descendants of Esau, became servants to David and Israel. This was a result of Esau trading away his birthright. We also see a similar thing in First Kings 11:15 when Joab kills all the males of Edom.

> *For it happened, when David was in Edom, and Joab*
> *the commander of the army had gone up to bury the*
> *slain, after he had killed every male in Edom.*

All the males of Edom were killed, which had a long-lasting generational effect upon that people. As a result of this action, there was no way to procreate this line of people. Why could these things happen? I believe this occurred because when Esau sold away the birthright, it gave the devil a right to take captive his book and the book of the nation of people that would come from him. The whole nation lost its destiny because of what the father of the nation had done and the trade he had made! These same things can happen to us as well. If someone in our history has done things that might have given the devil a legal right to claim our family line, our book could be held captive. We have to know how to go before the Courts of Heaven and get our book back and possess it. If there is anywhere in our family line someone that has "sold us out," our book is held captive.

There are two main signs I believe that can show that our book is held captive. The first sign is no matter how hard you try, you can't seem to have a sense of destiny. You have heard all the teachings and been told you were made for a purpose and are very special before God, but you still don't "feel" it. Instead of living life with a sense of purpose, you spend your life just doing good things. You may get excited about something for a while, but then you lose ambition. This can be a sign that you don't have your book.

The second sign is a familial history of debauchery, lust, and fleshly living. Proverbs 29:18 tells us that without a sense of destiny, people live recklessly.

> *Where there is no revelation, the people cast off*
> *restraint;*
> *But happy is he who keeps the law.*

If there is no real sense of purpose in life, then people will give themselves over to the lust of the flesh and all that is attached to it. Paul summed it up in First Corinthians 15:32.

> *If, in the manner of men, I have fought with beasts at*
> *Ephesus, what advantage is it to me? If the dead do*
> *not rise, "Let us eat and drink, for tomorrow we die!"*

Paul said if there is just this life, then what does it matter. Give yourself over to the flesh. There is no future. Enjoy the day in all its fleshly extravagance. There is no tomorrow. Of course, we know this isn't true. Yet if we don't have our book in which our destiny and purpose is written, then our family heritage could have been controlled by this philosophy. We must get back our book that has been taken captive. Once we do, there will be a sense of destiny that will overtake us.

In just a moment, I will give you a prayer to pray to get your book out of captivity and secure it. Before we get there, one more thing I would want you to be aware of is that angels can be involved in this process. Anywhere in Scripture where we see books being delivered to people it seems angels are prevalent. Revelation 10:8–9 shows an angel giving John a book to "eat."

> *Then the voice which I heard from heaven spoke to me again and said, "Go, take the little book which is open in the hand of the angel who stands on the sea and on the earth."*
>
> *So I went to the angel and said to him, "Give me the little book."*
>
> *And he said to me, "Take and eat it; and it will make your stomach bitter, but it will be as sweet as honey in your mouth."*

It seems that angels can be involved in the delivery of books to us. So as we begin to pray, be aware that angels are being dispatched to recover your book from wherever it may be. They can and will retrieve it and bring it back to you. The result will be a sense of destiny for you and your generations.

Here is a prayer to recover and secure your book that may have been taken captive.

 Lord, as I come to stand before Your Courts, I thank You that I have a book written in heaven concerning my destiny and future. I was created and made for a divine purpose. However, Lord, I sense that someone in my bloodline may have made a covenant with devilish powers that has allowed them to hold my book captive. Lord, as I stand before this Court, I am asking for my book back. I want the purpose that You made me for revealed and fulfilled.

Lord, as I stand before You, I repent for any and all covenants made with demon powers. Any agreements or covenants my ancestry has made with devilish powers I repent of. Any rights these covenants have given the powers of darkness to take captive my book, I am asking them to be annulled. I am sorry for any personal or generational involvement with demons and powers of darkness. I want nothing to do with them. I only want what is from You. Lord, I say before this Court that I am yours. The blood of Jesus has bought me, and as for me and my house, we shall serve the Lord! Lord, I also ask that my bloodline and I would be forgiven for any trust in or involvement or interaction with demon powers. I repent, Lord. I ask that the blood of Jesus according to Hebrews 12:24 would now speak on my behalf and undo any and every covenant that would empower demons to hold my book. I now want and decree my book freed. Lord, I also now want to return to these demon powers any claim they have on me. I want nothing of theirs. I only want what comes from You. You alone are my source, strength, and purpose for living.

I also, Lord, now dispatch angels to go and recover my book. Wherever my book might be held captive, I ask for it to be found and retrieved. I say before You that because of the blood of Jesus, every legal right of the devil to hold my book is now revoked and removed. The angels are now empowered and freed to recover my book and bring it to me! (At this time, you should be "looking" in the spirit. You might see, hear, sense an atmospheric change or other spiritual occurrences. These are the angels moving on your behalf. Keep "looking" and you may see your book being brought back to you.)

Lord, I thank You and receive my book for me and even my family line. Any and every book that belongs to me and that has been dedicated to my ancestry, I now receive. (Sometimes people "see" more than one book coming to them. Each of us has our own book. I have found, however, that the book for those in our family lines can be recovered as well. Also, if there are those who died prematurely and were unable to fulfill what was in their book, these books may also be retrieved. There are unfinished purposes within the family line that need to be stewarded into fullness.)

Lord, I thank You for the recovery and securing of my book. I receive it and dedicate myself to fulfilling all that was written about me before time began. I receive the grace that has already been given to me according to Second Timothy 1:9. Lord, let Your grace abound in me and through me to fulfill all You wrote in my book. Lord, I love You and thank You for this. In Jesus's name, Amen!

CHAPTER 9

OPENING THE
BOOKS OF DESTINY

ONCE we have our books recovered and we are in possession of them, they need to be opened. When you look through Scripture, you see books that are sealed or closed. You also see open books. Daniel 12:4 shows God instructing a book to be shut.

> But you, Daniel, shut up the words, and seal the book
> until the time of the end; many shall run to and fro,
> and knowledge shall increase.

There are times books are closed because of divine timing. There are other times, however, when books are shut, and unless they are opened, the purposes of God cannot be done. We see this in Revelation 5:1–4.

> *And I saw in the right hand of Him who sat on the throne a scroll written inside and on the back, sealed with seven seals. Then I saw a strong angel proclaiming with a loud voice, "Who is worthy to open the scroll and to loose its seals?" And no one in heaven or on the earth or under the earth was able to open the scroll, or to look at it.*
>
> *So I wept much, because no one was found worthy to open and read the scroll, or to look at it.*

This book needs to be opened for God's will and passion to be done. John is seen weeping because he knows that there is a need for this book to be opened so that God's purpose can be fulfilled on the earth. We know that Jesus, as the Lion of Judah and the Lamb of God, prevailed to open this book. However, the tears of John were essential to the opening of this book. Heaven was not toying with John's emotions. They needed his intercession to open this book.

Opened books are essential to the operations of the Courts of Heaven. Daniel 10:7 tells us the Courts' function is tied to open books.

A fiery stream issued
And came forth from before Him.
A thousand thousands ministered to Him;
Ten thousand times ten thousand stood before Him.
The court was seated,
And the books were opened.

The reason why the books must be opened is because cases are to be presented from these books. You cannot present a case from a book that is closed. When the books are opened, revelation of purpose and destiny can now flow freely. Many people have their books, but they are not open. We shared in the last chapter the signs that someone didn't have possession of their book. There are also signs that you have your book, but it is not open. There are basically two signs of this situation. The first is that you have a sense of destiny but do not know the specifics of it. You have this awareness that you were created for a purpose, yet you do not know the details of it. The second sign is connected to this one. You feel a deep sense of frustration and confusion. You want the destiny written in your book, but what you were created for is blurry and uncertain to you. Therefore, you have a great lack of discernment. You need your book open in the spirit realm so that the details of your destiny in your book can be known. This is seen in Isaiah 29:10–12 where there is no prophetic understanding and revelation because a book is sealed.

> *For the Lord has poured out on you*
> *The spirit of deep sleep,*
> *And has closed your eyes, namely, the prophets;*
> *And He has covered your heads, namely, the seers.*
>
> *The whole vision has become to you like the words of*
> *a book that is sealed, which men deliver to one who is*
> *literate, saying, "Read this, please."*
>
> *And he says, "I cannot, for it is sealed."*
>
> *Then the book is delivered to one who is illiterate,*
> *saying, "Read this, please."*
>
> *And he says, "I am not literate."*

The prophets have no revelation and the seers cannot see because of a book that is sealed. When we have our books but they are not open, there will be a lack of understanding, revelation, and discernment of what is in them. We must open these books. Once the books are open, not only will revelation be had, we will be able to present before the Courts of Heaven our case for the destiny we were made for.

There is one more thing we should know before we pray. When we approach the Courts of Heaven with opened books, we should present before the Courts our case based on purpose and not need. The reason the books are opened is because they are filled with the purpose God has for our lives. So as I approach His Courts, I am not bringing my needs to Him. I am declaring from the books the destiny He has written concerning my life and asking for it to be fulfilled. This can be very important in receiving from the Lord the release of destiny we were made for.

Here is a prayer we can pray to see the books of heaven concerning us opened.

Lord, as I come before Your Courts, I present myself before You. I thank You for all that Jesus has done for me that allows me to stand in this Holy Place. I declare from this place that You, Lord, are my Lord and King. I surrender to You all that I am. Thank You so much for loving me.

I thank You, Lord, for the book in heaven that is written about me. I thank You that I now possess this book. I ask now that this book would be opened and the revelation of Your purpose for my life would now come to me. I ask that anything that would cause my book to be shut and cause me confusion, frustration, and lack of detailed knowledge of my purpose be revoked and removed. I approach Your Courts with deep intercession. Just as Jesus was heard according to Hebrews 5:7 because of His fear of God, which manifested through tears of prayer and supplication, please let me be heard. I position myself before You and ask that my tears and cries be used by heaven to open the book concerning my destiny and future. Lord, would You allow heaven to regard my tears and intercession for the opening of my book. Just as John wept for the book to be opened in Revelation chapter 5, so I intercede with passion for my book to be open. Lord, I am desperate for Your will to be done in my life. I want only Your purpose accomplished.

Lord, as I see my book opened, I now come and stand before You to present from this opened book a case for my destiny to be fulfilled. According to Your purpose for me, I ask that it might manifest on the earth. Lord, I ask that You might be glorified and that Your purpose would be done. (Any detailed understanding you have concerning your destiny and purpose you should present before the

Lord here.) Lord, I lay aside anything that is of my own desires and not yours. Should what I want interfere with Your intent, I lay it before You. I say with Jesus according to Hebrews 5:7, "I come, O God, it is written of me in the volume of the book to do Your will!" Your will, Lord, is my passion. Please allow Your desires and purposes be fulfilled in me as they are written in the volume of the book in heaven. I love You, Lord, and lay my life before You in Your Courts. In Jesus's name, Amen!

CHAPTER 10

RESETTING TIMING IN THE COURTS OF HEAVEN

A S we endeavor to obtain our destiny and purpose from the Courts of Heaven, timing can be an issue. I do believe God has a specific timing for his purposes. However, I also believe the devil likes nothing better than to disrupt God's timing. We see this in Daniel 7:25–26.

He shall speak pompous words against the Most High,
Shall persecute the saints of the Most High,
And shall intend to change times and law.
Then the saints shall be given into his hand
For a time and times and half a time.

> *But the court shall be seated,*
> *And they shall take away his dominion,*
> *To consume and destroy it forever.*

One of the purposes of the Antichrist spirit today is to interrupt the timing of God (see 1 John 4:3). Daniel saw that this spirit would seek to change times and laws. The word "times" is the Hebrew word "zman," and it means an appointed time. In other words, it is a time appointed and designated for something to happen. All of us have had prophecies, awareness, and ideas about things God has promised us. We also have felt discouragement when these things did NOT happen within the time frame we felt was right. Sometimes this happens because we simply weren't sensitive to the timing of God. Other times however, the devil has been successful in disrupting this timing. When this happens, what the Bible calls a "sick heart" can develop because of hope deferred. Proverbs 13:12 refers to this "sick heart" that comes from hopes and dreams being dashed time and again.

> *Hope deferred makes the heart sick,*
> *But when the desire comes, it is a tree of life.*

The devil's ability to mess with the timing of God in regards to dreams and their prophetic fulfillment will cause this "sick heart." The result is that no real vital faith functions within us. We may even still be serving the Lord, but the pain of really believing in something and seeing it fail again is too much to endure. We, therefore, shift into a "safe" posture in the spirit and ignore our emotions to protect ourselves from the hurt of another letdown. These moments can happen because the devil disrupted the timing of God. That which was supposed to happen didn't occur at the appointed time. Therefore, everything got thrown out of sync and out of its divine orbit. One of the big issues this raises is the sovereignty of God. Many people have what I call a "hyper view" of God's sovereignty. Their attitude is that if something happens, it must therefore be the will of God. They fail to recognize, however, that there is a very real devil seeking to interrupt God's will. There can, in fact, be a passion of God that is not realized because the devil disrupted God's desires. Paul spoke of this in First Thessalonians 2:18.

> *Therefore we wanted to come to you—even I, Paul, time and again—but Satan hindered us.*

Paul didn't say it was God's will. He said it was satan that hindered him and his timing. This is important because otherwise we make room for the devil to mess with the timing of God as a result of our theological position. When we have a hyper view of the sovereignty of God, it creates a passivity that satan can exploit. We must repent for a misguided view of God's sovereignty that has allowed the devil to exploit God's purposes and us. The result is that the timing of God is frustrated.

There are several occasions in Scripture where this happened. The main one I see is Israel coming out of their captivity in Egypt. In Genesis 15:13–14, we see God telling Abraham how long Israel will be in captivity.

> *Then He said to Abram: "Know certainly that your descendants will be strangers in a land that is not theirs, and will serve them, and they will afflict them four hundred years. And also the nation whom they serve I will judge; afterward they shall come out with great possessions."*

Abraham is told that Israel, his descendants, will be there for 400 years. However, by the time they come out of captivity in Exodus 12:40–41, they were there 430 years.

*Now the sojourn of the children of Israel who lived
in Egypt was four hundred and thirty years. And it
came to pass at the end of the four hundred and thirty
years—on that very same day—it came to pass that
all the armies of the LORD went out from the land of
Egypt.*

According to the timing of the Lord, they were to be
in Egypt 400 years. Clearly however, something allowed
this time to be lengthened to 430 years. We might look at
this story and think, "What is the big deal?" However, people who would have seen freedom might have died within
those 30 additional years of captivity. There were those
who would have been young who were instead old. Instead
of enjoying liberty, these people suffered under cruel, hard
bondage for another 30 years. The time of their deliverance
came and went, and they were still in captivity. The devil
had been able to disrupt the timing of God. This is one of his
main strategic efforts. Through this, he causes a "sick heart"
to develop when the promises spoken over our lives never
happen. We need to know how to reset the timing of God
when we encounter any interruption. Notice that in Daniel's encounter with God, it was the Courts of Heaven that
dealt with the devil's attempt to mess with the appointed
times. The Antichrist spirit's dominion and authority was

revoked and removed. This stopped the disruption of God's timing and reset it. This is what God promised in Joel 2:25.

> *So I will restore to you the years that the swarming*
> *locust has eaten,*
> *The crawling locust,*
> *The consuming locust,*
> *And the chewing locust,*
> *My great army which I sent among you.*

Notice the promise is to restore the years. Obviously, this doesn't mean the literal time of years. It does, however, mean the *productivity* of those years. God is declaring that He will restore goods, finances, life, health, and anything else that was lost or devoured. He will give back what should have been accumulated over the course of the years within a very short time. There will be, in essence, the restoration of the years. What you should have had at this time, you will still have. Instead of it accumulating over years, it will come supernaturally into your life in a quick span. This occurs because we know how to go before the Courts of Heaven and reset the timing of God in our lives. When the Court was seated, the effort of the devil to interrupt timing was frustrated.

If you feel this applies to you, then you should come before the Courts of Heaven and present your case for the restoration of the years that have been devoured. Perhaps it is in regards to children, relationships, marriage, health, finances, prophetic destinies, and/or influence. Whatever it is, we can stand before His Courts and ask for this resetting of time. The result will be a reordering of the spirit and a revoking of demonic interference. You will be set back into divine orbit and in sync with God's passion for your life. The desire shall come, and it will be a tree of life you will eat from to fulfillment and deep satisfaction (see Proverbs 13:12).

Here is a prayer to approach God's Courts and request this resetting of time in your life and His purposes in and through you.

Lord, I come before Your Courts and ask, on the basis of Jesus and His blood, that I be accepted. I thank You that I can stand before You because I am the righteousness of God in Christ Jesus. Thank You so much for all You have done for me.

As I stand before Your Courts, I know that the devil has messed with Your timing in my life. I am aware that he has been able to disrupt the fulfillment of prophetic promises I carry. I know that dreams in my heart that have come from You have yet to be fulfilled. I ask that all You have spoken concerning me would not fall to the ground, but would become reality. I yield my heart before You and surrender. I want all that You have designed for me to happen. Please, Lord, let Your will be done in my life and in all that concerns me. I bring these promises to You specifically. (Recite before the Lord any words you have, promises you carry, and/or dreams for your life.) Lord, I am asking that I could apprehend this that I was made for. Thank You so much.

I ask, Lord, that the years that have been lost through the disruption of timing would now be restored. I ask on the basis of Joel 2:25 that everything that has been lost, destroyed, or devoured would now be recovered. I am asking You, Lord, for the productivity of the years to be given back to me and my generations. You are the God of restoration and recovery. I am asking of You and before Your Courts for this to occur.

I also ask, Lord, that should there be any legal issue in the spirit that the devil would be using to resist me, that Your blood would speak for me according to Hebrews 12:24. I repent for any wrong or rebellious decisions that allowed the devil to steal my promises or future. I ask that his case against me would be revoked. I also repent for any wrong view of the sovereignty of God. Any area of my life in which I have not taken responsibility because of this wrong view, I repent. Forgive me, Lord, for this and allow the blood of Jesus to please speak for me. Any place there might be covenants with devilish powers from my bloodlines, I ask that these would be annulled. I thank You for the power of the blood. Lord, should there be anything else that satan would use to resist what is in my book of destiny, I ask that you might show it to me that I might ask for the blood to speak on my behalf. Lord, I stand before You and open my bloodline and myself to Your examination. (At this point, be sensitive in the spirit. Anything you see, feel, hear, and/or discern, just present it to the Lord and ask for the blood to speak on your behalf.)

Lord, now on the basis of who You are and what You have provided, I ask and decree that all the resistance of the devil against my future and destiny is revoked. I say from Your Courts that any and every legal right against me according to Colossians 2:14 is now nailed to the cross. I am free to see time reset, dreams fulfilled, years restored, and prophetic destiny realized. I receive it from the very Courts of Heaven and move into it in Jesus's name. Amen!

CHAPTER 11

STEPPING ONTO THE TRADING FLOORS OF HEAVEN

THERE is a dimension in the heavenly realm we call *trading floors*. To understand this concept, we need to look back to before the beginning of time. There was activity in the heavenly realm, which, when we understand it, can help us know how to see things shift in the Courts of Heaven. Ezekiel 28:14–16 reveals some of this activity. In this passage, God laments lucifer's fall.

You were the anointed cherub who covers;
I established you;
You were on the holy mountain of God;
You walked back and forth in the midst of fiery stones.

*You were perfect in your ways from the day you were
created,
Till iniquity was found in you.*

*By the abundance of your trading
You became filled with violence within,
And you sinned;
Therefore I cast you as a profane thing
Out of the mountain of God;
And I destroyed you, O covering cherub,
From the midst of the fiery stones.*

Before the enemy was satan on the earth, he was an
angelic being known as lucifer in heaven. Isaiah 14:12–14
shows him losing his place in heaven.

*How you are fallen from heaven,
O Lucifer, son of the morning!
How you are cut down to the ground,
You who weakened the nations!*

*For you have said in your heart:
"I will ascend into heaven,
I will exalt my throne above the stars of God;
I will also sit on the mount of the congregation
On the farthest sides of the north;*

I will ascend above the heights of the clouds,
I will be like the Most High."

We see in Ezekiel that lucifer was involved in *trading* in heaven. Even though this passage is about the King of Tyre in the natural realm, God is also disclosing truths concerning the fall of lucifer from heaven. This is commonly understood in most circles. When you read this passage, it would at first glance seem to indicate trading was wrong. However, this was lucifer/satan's activity while in a heavenly realm. The truth is it wasn't trading that was wrong. It was trading with a polluted heart and impure intent that made what he did wrong. Trading is, in fact, a heavenly/spiritual activity. We know this because this is what Jesus actually did on the cross. He made a trade on our behalf. Second Corinthians 5:21 tells us He took His righteousness and traded it for our sin.

For He made Him who knew no sin to be sin for us,
that we might become the righteousness of God in
Him.

Through a trade, we have been made righteous. We have a right to stand in His presence and His Courts because of the trade Jesus made on our behalf. It doesn't end there, however. We are also healed because of the trade of Jesus. Isaiah 54:3 tells us that Jesus took our sickness so we could be well.

> *Surely He has borne our griefs*
> *And carried our sorrows;*
> *Yet we esteemed Him stricken,*
> *Smitten by God, and afflicted.*

The word "griefs" is the Hebrew word "choliy," and it means disease, sickness, and calamity. The word "sorrows" is the Hebrew word "makob," and it means pain. When Jesus hung on the cross, which is what the prophet Isaiah is seeing, He was actually making a trade for us. He was taking our sickness, diseases, and pains and giving us health, wholeness, and wellness. Receiving healing is a result of embracing the trade Jesus made for us on the cross. There is at least one more part of the trade Jesus made for us on the cross as well. He took poverty that we might be rich. Second Corinthians 8:9 tells us that He became poor that we might be rich!

> *For you know the grace of our Lord Jesus Christ, that*
> *though He was rich, yet for your sakes He became*
> *poor, that you through His poverty might become rich.*

Through the trade of Jesus on the cross, the spirit of poverty has no right to possess us. We have a right based on Jesus's trade to be prosperous, wealthy, and rich.

I am showing this to let you know that *trading* is a spiritual activity. Lucifer's trading in heaven was not an evil thing. It is actually the activity of heaven and the spirit realm. Let me show you one other verse that can help us understand this. Isaiah 61:3 shows the power of trading. We are called by God

> *To console those who mourn in Zion,*
> *To give them beauty for ashes,*
> *The oil of joy for mourning,*
> *The garment of praise for the spirit of heaviness;*
> *That they may be called trees of righteousness,*
> *The planting of the LORD, that He may be glorified.*

As a result of the trade Jesus made, we can take our ashes and trade them for His beauty. We can take our spirit of heaviness and trade it for a garment of praise. We can take our mourning and trade it for the oil of joy. Notice that as we progressively and habitually do this, we become trees of righteousness that display His splendor. In other words, through trading, we are transformed into His image and likeness. As we learn how to step onto the trading floors of the spirit realm, we can become all we were meant to be. His power works in us gloriously to transform us. Wow! What a powerful principle.

To see how this connects to the Courts of Heaven, we must understand where the *trading floors* are in heavenly places. Notice in Ezekiel chapter 28 that lucifer existed in the "holy mountain of God on the fiery stones." He was then removed from this place because of his improper trading. When the Bible speaks of the "holy mountain of God," it is speaking of a spiritual dimension, not a physical place. Hebrews 12:22 tells us where we are in the spirit.

> *But you have come to Mount Zion and to the city of the living God, the heavenly Jerusalem, to an innumerable company of angels.*

We are now in and have come to "Mount Zion." This is another reference to "the holy mountain of God." In other words, we are now spiritually in the same place that satan was cast out of. This is one of the reasons why he hates us so much. We now have access to the very spiritual place he once occupied. This spiritual realm that the scripture calls "Mount Zion" is also the place of the Courts of Heaven.

In Hebrews 12:22–24, we see this dimension is a judicial arena.

> *But you have come to Mount Zion and to the city of the living God, the heavenly Jerusalem, to an innumerable company of angels, to the general assembly and church of the firstborn who are registered in heaven, to God the Judge of all, to the spirits of just men made perfect, to Jesus the Mediator of the new covenant, and to the blood of sprinkling that speaks better things than that of Abel.*

So much of the spiritual activity that is mentioned here is legal in nature. For instance, the word "church" is the Greek word "ecclesia," and it speaks of a judicial, legislative, and governmental body. The ecclesia or the church has the right to stand in the Courts of Heaven. God is revealed as the Judge of all. This is a legal place. The "spirits of just men" is a reference to the Great Cloud Of Witnesses. Witnesses are a judicial term for those who give testimony. Jesus as the Mediator of the new covenant defines legal terms. The "blood that speaks" describes that which is giving testimony. So Mount Zion or the holy mountain of God is a judicial place within which the Courts of Heaven function. Satan as lucifer in this place made *trades* on the fiery stones.

So *trading* is an activity in the Courts of Heaven. This is what Noah did when he came out of the ark in Genesis 8:20–22. He built an altar or a trading floor and released a soothing sacrifice to God.

> *Then Noah built an altar to the LORD, and took*
> *of every clean animal and of every clean bird, and*
> *offered burnt offerings on the altar. And the LORD*
> *smelled a soothing aroma. Then the LORD said in His*
> *heart, "I will never again curse the ground for man's*
> *sake, although the imagination of man's heart is evil*
> *from his youth; nor will I again destroy every living*
> *thing as I have done.*
>
> > *While the earth remains,*
> > *Seedtime and harvest,*
> > *Cold and heat,*
> > *Winter and summer,*
> > *And day and night*
> > *Shall not cease."*

As God received the offering/trade of Noah, it moved Him to make a judicial decree. He freed the earth from a curse and set it in order.

We, too, as those appointed for the Courts of Heaven, can stand on the trading floors of the fiery stones. We can stand there by faith and enter the trade Jesus made. We can also by faith make trades in these realms where God's heart is moved and judicial decrees can be made. We have a right to stand in these holy places and operate there. Trading in the spiritual world is a spiritual part of the Courts of Heaven. When Noah offered up his sacrifice, it wasn't the stench of burning flesh in the natural that moved God. It was, however, the aroma of Noah's heart in the midst of the offering that touched the heart of God. That which was released in the natural moved things in the spiritual.

I want to mention a couple of ways we can trade once we are standing in these places. We can take the brokenness of our life and trade it for His wholeness. We can take our ashes and, by faith, trade for His beauty. We can take our mourning and trade for His oil of joy. We can take any and all heaviness and trade it for a garment of praise. As we enter the trading floors, we can make these transactions.

Also, we can take our finances and trade them as well. Our finances are an expression of who we are and our heart to the Lord. This is what Paul said in Second Corinthians 8:5. He rejoiced that the Corinthian church gave what they had,

> *And not only as we had hoped, but they first gave*
> *themselves to the Lord, and then to us by the will of*
> *God.*

Paul said what they gave was an expression of their heart, which they had already given to the Lord. So when we stand on the trading floors of heaven and bring our offering, we are actually giving an expression of our life and our heart. This is what Noah did. God smelled the soothing aroma of his offering. It wasn't the stench of burning animal flesh but rather the aroma of Noah's heart. This moved the judicial heart of God. There are times when we can step on the trading floors of the Courts of Heaven and make trades/offerings that can shift things in our lives. However, as the ecclesia of God, we can also make trades that can free culture and see God's passion fulfilled.

Should you desire to step onto the trading floors of heaven, here is a prayer you can pray to see this realm opened and to begin witnessing trades.

 Lord, I thank You for the trading floors of heaven that are a part of the Courts of Heaven. Thank You for the understanding that in these places, we can make "trades"

that can shift spiritual realms. Thank You for the honor of standing in these places with You.

Lord, as I come upon these trading floors I do so in the fear of the Lord and with an awareness of Your holiness. I am aware, Lord, that my only right to stand here is because of Jesus and what He has done for me. So with great confidence in the work of Jesus on my behalf, I now stand in this place. I also stand here in a posture of faith. Thank You, Lord, that You give me the right to make trades in this place and to secure from You all that Jesus died for me to have.

Lord, the first thing I do is enter into the trade that Jesus made for me. Lord, I thank You that because of Jesus's trade, I am considered the righteousness of God in Christ Jesus. With great boldness, I take this place and cast away any sense of unworthiness that would try and cling to me. I say, according to the word of God, that I have been made worthy by the blood to stand on these trading floors. I also say that because of Jesus's trade for me, I am healed and whole physically, emotionally, spiritually, and in every other way. I take for myself the wholeness Jesus died for me to have. I also say that I cast away all poverty connected to me. According to the trade Jesus made for me, I am rich. Lord, I enter into all the wealth, prosperity, and riches that are mine in Jesus's name.

Lord, I also now bring any trade of finances that expresses my heart for You. I come to stand on the trading floors of heaven before You and honor You with the finances that represent my heart. Just as Noah offered the animals as an expression of his heart, I offer this money to You. Lord, would You allow these finances to speak before You on my behalf as You receive them upon the fiery stones of heaven. Just as the smoke of Noah's offering touched Your heart from that trading floor, would You allow the smoke of the incense of this offering to touch Your heart as well. Lord, I am asking that this trade would allow this request (be specific about what you are asking the Lord for) to be heard. I am asking, Lord, for a shift in the realm of the spirit to bring breakthrough in my life.

Thank You so much, Lord, for allowing me to stand on these trading floors of heaven. It is with great honor, faith, and fear of the Lord that I function in this place. In Jesus's name. Amen!

CHAPTER 12

RECEIVING HEALING FROM THE COURTS OF HEAVEN

HEALING is provided through what Jesus did for us on the cross. His atoning work put things legally in place for us to be made well from every physical disease. This is why Peter in First Peter 2:24 declares we *were* healed by what Jesus did for us on the cross. He reveals Jesus,

> *Who Himself bore our sins in His own body on the tree, that we, having died to sins, might live for righteousness—by whose stripes you were healed.*

This means that we no longer are trying to convince God to heal us. He, in fact, has already set everything in place that would be necessary for us to be healed. Any struggle we now have comes from our inability to step into the realm of faith where healing occurs. Isaiah 53:4 tells us the legal work Jesus took up on our behalf.

Surely He has borne our griefs
And carried our sorrows;
Yet we esteemed Him stricken,
Smitten by God, and afflicted.

As we have said in a previous chapter of this book, the word "griefs" is best translated as "disease and sickness." The word "sorrows" can be translated as "pain." So when Jesus died on the cross, there was a legal transaction that occurred. In the spirit, He made sickness and disease an illegal thing for the believer. Those who are in covenant with Him have a right to be healed and made whole. This is what Jesus said in Mark 7:26–27 while dealing with the Syro-Phoenician woman as she sought healing and deliverance for her daughter.

The woman was a Greek, a Syro-Phoenician by birth,
and she kept asking Him to cast the demon out of her

daughter. But Jesus said to her, "Let the children be
filled first, for it is not good to take the children's bread
and throw it to the little dogs."

Jesus said healing is the children's bread. In other words,
it is the covenant right of those who belong to the Lord.
This was actually a reference to the Old Covenant. We
know that this is contained in the New Covenant and even
more so because it is made on better promises (see Hebrews
8:6). So when Jesus died on the cross, He set in place legally
everything that is rightfully ours in regards to healing. The
Holy Spirit, however, is the One who executes everything
Jesus legally purchased for us. John 16:8-11 tells us one of
the functions of the Holy Spirit. Jesus says to His disciples
that when the Spirit comes,

He will convict the world of judgment, because the
ruler of this world is judged.

The Holy Spirit convinces and persuades us of the judgment Jesus rendered on the cross. He then empowers us as
the legal officers to execute all that Jesus died for us to have.
Through the anointing of the Holy Spirit, we see applied
everything Jesus legally purchased for us. The one problem is that the devil as the adversary will seek to contend

against us in our attempts to receive our healing. If there are issues in our own life or bloodline, the devil will seek to stop us from having what is rightfully ours. Just a little further insight might help us understand this. Remember that in First Peter 5:8 we talked about the legal function of the devil.

> *Be sober, be vigilant; because your adversary the devil walks about like a roaring lion, seeking whom he may devour.*

The adversary is the "antidikos" or one who brings a lawsuit. Satan as our adversary is seeking to build legal cases against us in the spirit. This allows him the right to devour us. This definitely includes sickness. As I have now traveled for years teaching on the legal realms of the spirit and the Courts of Heaven, the main question and contention I face is the idea that Jesus FINISHED the work. I am told that the devil no longer has a right to resist us and definitely not to stand legally against us. I am confronted with this idea over and over. HERE IS THE PROBLEM WITH THAT ARGUMENT! Peter, the great New Testament apostle, didn't believe this. Peter said, we must be on guard and diligent not to give the devil a legal right to build a case, bring a lawsuit, and devour us. If satan has found a legal case, then we need to know how to undo it. Peter clearly was under the persuasion that the devil, as our legal opponent, devoured us with sickness and other afflictions because he was bringing a lawsuit. We know this is true because of the term Peter used to describe the devil and his function! Lest you misunderstand, I DO BELIEVE Jesus FINISHED the work…LEGALLY. However, what Jesus did legally has to be executed through the anointing of the Holy Spirit for us to receive the benefits. This means we must not be ignorant of how the Holy Spirit moves and operates. Paul mentions this in First Corinthians 12:1.

> *Now concerning spiritual gifts, brethren, I do not want you to be ignorant.*

Paul exhorted us not to be ignorant of the spirit realm and how it operates. It is the Holy Spirit through the anointing that executes all Jesus died for. The Holy Spirit does this through people who have learned to yield and move in agreement with Him. This is imperative to move out of the way anything the devil would be using legally to resist our healing.

This can involve undoing any case the devil would be using to bring a lawsuit against us. To get an even deeper understanding of this, please know that the Greek word "antidikos," translated as "adversary," comes from two words. "Anti" means to deny, be against or instead of. "Dikos" means rights. So the devil would bring a lawsuit in the spirit realm to *deny you what is rightfully yours.* In other words, satan brings a case against us to stop us from getting the breakthroughs Jesus legally set in place for us. We have to know how to go before the Courts of Heaven, undo any and every case, and receive the fullness of what is ours because of Jesus and His sacrifice. If you would like a more detailed perspective of how the Courts of Heaven operate in regards to healing, you should read my book, *Receiving Healing From The Courts Of Heaven.*

When dealing with legal issues that could be stopping healing, we must know there could be issues in our personal lives and/or bloodlines as well. I find that most people, once they are aware of something personal, will deal with it. However the bloodline issues can be a little more difficult. This is primarily because we do not know what might be in our bloodline that would allow the enemy to bring sickness upon us. Asking God for any revelation that the devil might be using can be very helpful. The Lord is faithful in showing us issues that satan is legally working against us. It is also helpful to pray with a person who has a prophetic/seer gift so they might help discern what is the devil's legal strategy. You can find a list of seer gifts among our HUBS at www.globalreformer.com. You can contact them, and they will be glad to help in this process. Another thing that can be done is to simply use Colossians 2:14. In this verse is a stated verdict of the cross. Through Jesus's act on the cross, God made us alive,

> *Having wiped out the handwriting of requirements that was against us, which was contrary to us. And He has taken it out of the way, having nailed it to the cross.*

We by faith take this verdict and execute it into place by the power of the Holy Spirit. We ask and decree that all Jesus has done for us on the cross is now working and speaking on our behalf. Once we silence any accusation against us, we then ask for the healing power of Jesus to touch and move in us. When any legal right of the devil is revoked, all Jesus died for will come into our lives. Thank You, Jesus, for all You have done.

Here is a prayer to receive healing from the Courts of Heaven.

Lord, as I stand before You in Your Courts, I thank You that You are the healer. You are the One who makes all things new and whole. I thank You for all that Jesus did on the cross to carry away sickness and bear away pains. Everything that was legally necessary, Jesus has done for me. Thank You, Lord, so much.

I also recognize, Lord, that there is an adversary that would legally want to resist all You died for me to have. Even in the Old Testament in Psalm 103:3, You are the One who forgives all my iniquities and heals all my diseases. Lord, I thank you that any iniquity that would speak against me is silenced by Your blood. Thank You that Your blood deals with any sin in my personal life, but also every iniquity in my bloodline that afflicts me.

Lord, I come and lay my life down and surrender to You. Any attitude in me of stubbornness, rebellion, and iniquity, would You reveal to me. If there is a legal right the devil is using to hold me in sickness, please let it be known. (At this point listen, look, and be sensitive to anything you might sense. Anything revealed, repent and ask for the blood of Jesus to speak for you. Be aware that there may be a slight whisper in the "back of your mind" telling you why God will not answer you. Acknowledge this and repent.)

Lord, as I stand before Your Courts, I want to remind this Court of what Jesus has done. According to Colossians 2:14, every accusation and case against me Jesus took out of the way, nailing it to His cross. I ask and decree that all that Jesus has done for me now speaks for me. Any bloodline issue that I know or that is unknown is now revoked by the work of Jesus on the cross. It can no longer be used to hold me in sickness. I am free through repentance as I agree with the blood of Jesus that is speaking for me.

I now ask for the power and anointing of the Holy Spirit to take all that Jesus has done on the cross and execute it in my life. I receive the anointing of the Spirit. I ask for the healing flow now to touch me and execute judgment against any and all sickness in my body. I decree from the Courts of Heaven that sickness is illegal and it has no right to cling to me. I receive the touch of Jesus through the Holy Spirit that now causes sickness to dry up and be removed. I declare I am healed and free from every disease and sickness in Jesus's name! Thank You so much, Jesus, for Your healing life that now flows into my body. Amen.

CHAPTER 13

UNLOCKING WEALTH FROM THE COURTS OF HEAVEN

DEUTERONOMY 8:18 makes the statement that has fashioned the cry of a church for generations. It is the cry for wealth that would empower us to see God's purposes done on the earth. This is actually what is recorded in this verse.

And you shall remember the LORD your God, for it is He who gives you power to get wealth, that He may establish His covenant which He swore to your fathers, as it is this day.

God's passion is revealed in this verse. He wants to give the *power to get wealth* so His purposes might be done on the earth. Please notice it is the power to get wealth and not wealth itself. God will give favor, ideas, concepts, and position, but we must parlay that into wealth. We cannot see God's will done in the cultures of the earth without wealth to sustain it. God loves all people. However, what He will do on the earth requires wealthy people through whom to do it. With this promise and decree, we see a paradox. Even though this is the desire of the Lord, we see many in the body of Christ struggling under a spirit of poverty, lack, and insufficiency. This must be removed so the purposes of God can be done.

Some in the church would condemn, scrutinize, and criticize anyone who would say wealth is necessary. They would caution us to be careful of the *"love of money which is the root of all kinds of evil"* (1 Timothy 6:10). I would point out, however, that it is the *love* of money and not money itself that is evil. The Lord is very capable of doing a work in our heart so we can steward the riches of this world for His kingdom purpose on the earth without allowing them to own us. If the purpose of God is to be seen and fulfilled on the earth, then there must be money to accomplish it. Even the winning of the lost costs money. Crusades, events, seminars, and other functions all require money. Factor in then the reformation of culture, and you have a billion-dollar agenda. My point is the work of the Gospel is not cheap. The promise of the Lord is that He would give the power to get wealth to see His covenant purposes accomplished. It must mean then that the Lord desires to transfer His people from not enough and just enough to more than enough and overflowing wealth.

Not only is this the desire of the Lord for His purposes on the earth to be done, but He also wants His people blessed. There is nothing more debilitating than the oppression of lack. Mary and I have lived in that state in times gone by. It wasn't fun or pretty. It puts stresses and strains on everything. Through consistent faithfulness to the principles of God however, we have seen the blessing of God come on our lives. In the midst of the hard times, God always met us. Now we have transitioned into a more blessed life. There were times when we were just surviving. We knew, however, that God wanted to bless us so we could be a blessing. This is a part of our rights as the seed of Abraham (see Genesis 12:2). The key to us coming into this place was the discovery of the Courts of Heaven. In chapter 9, I talked about the resetting of time from the Courts of Heaven. This is key to us seeing prosperity and blessings come. When the devil has been able to disrupt the timing of God, it throws everything out of sync. Usually, one of the things that is affected is finances. Quite often, when we are in the center of God's timing, everything is working well, and money is available to us. However, if things get out of order and the timing is messed up, finances can be affected in a negative way. The flow of funds can be cut off or, at least, seemingly squeezed to a trickle. We must go before the Courts of Heaven and begin to reset the timing.

The other element that can stop financial blessings from coming into our life is the principle of the trading floors that I shared in chapter 10. I want to unleash a principle here that can help us get wealth working on our behalf. In Matthew 20:1–16, we see the story of those who were hired to labor in a vineyard. First of all, wherever you work, that is a trading floor. You trade your time for wages. So when someone is hired to work somewhere, they are stepping onto the trading floor of that company. If you read the story, you will find the first group went on the basis of *agreement*. In other words, they had a contract to protect themselves so they got their days' worth of pay. All other groups hired throughout the day went on the basis of *whatever is right!* This group trusted the goodness, generosity, and liberality of the landowner. The first group was religious legalists. They labored and got what was agreed to. The other groups served out of and from grace. The last group, for instance, who worked only an hour got the same pay as the ones who worked all day. The question here is *what trading floor are you functioning on?* It wasn't about *what* they did. They all worked in the same vineyard. It was about *where* they did it from in the spirit realm. What trading floor were they functioning from? We can function in the spirit from the trading floor of agreement/legalism, or we can function from the trading floor of grace. Again, it is not about what we are doing, but where we are doing it from. The end result was that great increase and prosperity came to those who functioned on the trading floor of grace. Just one point from the story shows the drastic difference. In Matthew 20:15, the landowner condemns the legalists grumbling, asking them,

> *Is it not lawful for me to do what I wish with my own things? Or is your eye evil because I am good?*

As the laborers came to get their pay, the generosity of the landowner was revealed. Those who had agreed (the legalists) became upset and offended. They murmured because the ones who had labored only an hour got the same pay. The response of the landowner is classic. He said, "Is your eye evil because I am good?" In essence, he says, "Is the goodness of my heart causing the evil in yours to be revealed?" Wow. God is looking for those who will get off the trading floors of legalism and onto the trading floors of grace. He is looking for those through whom He can manifest His goodness, generosity, liberality, and kindness, and the religious have a problem with that.

Let me show you how this understanding came to me. My practice in prayer had been to carefully list in detail what I needed from the Lord financially. I had done this for years. God had always met what I asked for. One day, the Lord said to me while I was praying, "Stop agreeing with Me." I knew instantly He was talking about this story in Matthew chapter 20. I began at that moment to stop listing my detailed needs. I simply began to pray and say, "I serve You on the basis of whatever is right." Instantly, finances began to increase. Multiplication started to come. I was doing the same thing I had always done. However, I was now doing it from a different place in the spirit. Yet that simple, little adjustment in my prayer changed everything. It wasn't until later that I realized I had stepped off the trading floors of legalism and onto the trading floors of grace. New realms of prosperity began to come as I labored and made trades from this place of grace.

I want to help you reset timing in regards to your finances. I also want to help you get off the trading floors of legalism and onto the trading floors of grace. As you do, I believe the power to get wealth will be released to you.

Restrictions that have stifled you can be removed, and new levels of fruitfulness can come.

This prayer can help this process and release new realms of wealth from the Courts of Heaven.

Lord, I stand before Your Courts to ask for the power to get wealth. Your Word promises that if I will remember you, that You would give me the power to see wealth birthed. Lord, I come first asking for this wealth for Your kingdom's will to be done. You promised in Your Word that if I would seek first Your kingdom, all other things would be added to me. This is according to Matthew 6:33. Lord, I come and lay down my life and my desires and say that my passion is to see wealth produced so Your covenant can be established on the earth. I thank You, Lord, that You purify my heart so that I might have the right motives concerning wealth. I also ask, however, that blessings would come to my family. I ask that You would make me a good steward of what You trust me with. Work in me so that I am prepared to be entrusted with wealth and all that is connected to it.

Lord, I realize that the devil's disrupting of timing can cause lack and not allow me to have what You intended to be in my hand. Just as I prayed earlier concerning this interruption of timing, I repent for any place I have allowed the devil legal right to do this. I ask for Your blood to speak for me and remove his rights to operate. Please forgive me for rebellion, unwise decisions, a hyper view of Your sovereignty, and any other thing the devil would be using to accuse me. I ask that his rights be revoked before Your Courts. Lord, You are jealous for me to be wealthy for Your kingdom purposes to be done. I yield to You and ask for mercy for my life and bloodline. Thank You, Lord, for resetting your timing and bringing to me the restoration of the years. Thank You that productivity is now restored to me.

I also, Lord, come to stand on the trading floors of grace in Your Courts. Lord, forgive me for being a legalist and agreeing with You. I say I now serve You on the basis of whatever is right. I step off the trading floors of legalism and onto the trading floors of grace. I ask, Lord, that as I stand here, that Your goodness will be made manifest in me. Lord, let my life be one You can use to challenge others' views of You. Lord, awaken in me a new awareness of how good You really are. Let my life be a display of the generosity of God personified. Thank You so much, Lord. From this time on, I serve, I give, and I obey from the trading floors of grace. In Jesus's name, Amen.

CHAPTER 14

THE COURTS OF HEAVEN AND THE SEVEN MOUNTAINS

IN the church, many have become aware of what is called the *Seven Mountains of Culture*. This is a term to describe spheres of influence that determine what society looks like. They also have been referred to as the *molders of culture*. The influence of these *Seven Mountains* shape the thoughts, culture, and worldview of a society. If we are to see a cultural transformation of society so not only are masses born again, but society itself begins to reflect the kingdom of God, these *Mountains* must be altered from their present state. These seven spheres of society are religion, family, education, business, government, arts/entertainment, and media. The sound and voice coming from these mountains/

spheres are to be reformed. The result would be the changing of the worldview to that which is more in line with the kingdom of God. The way I put it is that life in the nations would look more like heaven than like hell. We are here to see the kingdoms of this world become the kingdoms of our Lord and Christ (see Revelation 11:15). Jesus said in Matthew 25:31–32 that there will be a nation of sheep and a nation of goats.

> *When the Son of Man comes in His glory, and all the*
> *holy angels with Him, then He will sit on the throne*
> *of His glory. All the nations will be gathered before*
> *Him, and He will separate them one from another, as*
> *a shepherd divides his sheep from the goats.*

The sheep nation will be those people groups who have been radically affected by the Gospel of the kingdom. Their culture will be altered to agree with the standards, morals, ethics, values, and virtues of the King, Jesus! The goat nation, on the other hand, will be those who have adopted another worldview and are standing against God and His agenda for the nations. It is the job of the ecclesia or church to see its nation discipled into sheep. Jesus tells us in Matthew 28:19 what His church, the ecclesia, should accomplish.

Go therefore and make disciples of all the nations,
baptizing them in the name of the Father and of the
Son and of the Holy Spirit.

Making disciples of nations does not involve just getting individuals saved. Making disciples of nations means shifting culture to agree with our King and the kingdom. This is why Jesus's passion is to seek and save what is lost. We find this in Luke 19:10.

For the Son of Man has come to seek and to save that
which was lost.

Notice that Jesus didn't say to seek and save who was lost but rather *that which was lost*. Redemption is not just for people. God desires to redeem all things, including the culture of societies and nations. This is where the Seven Mountains of Culture come in. Influencing these realms will allow nations to shift back to the God-ordained purpose written in the books before time began. This is what we as an ecclesia in our nations are responsible for. Early in this book, we talked about our individual books of destiny. We must realize, though, that anything that has a kingdom purpose has a book in heaven about it. This includes nations and cultures. Revelation 10:10–11 shows John receiving a book from an angel and eating it. This is a way of saying that John was receiving heavenly revelation concerning nations. We know this because after the book is eaten, John is able to prophesy to nations.

> *Then I took the little book out of the angel's hand and ate it, and it was as sweet as honey in my mouth. But when I had eaten it, my stomach became bitter. And he said to me, "You must prophesy again about many peoples, nations, tongues, and kings."*

Clearly, what was in the book concerned peoples, nations, tongues, and kings. This was why John was being empowered to prophesy about them. The book he ate had the destiny and concerns of nations in it. I believe what was in the book was the destiny and kingdom order of God for particular nations. It contained revelations of the divine desire for the nations of the world. This is important because this is what we are to see nations transformed into. We are to see what was written in the book of nations before time began to be fleshed out on the earth. Nations are not to be fashioned and formed in the image of what we think. Nations are to be fashioned and formed into the image of what God wrote in their book.

For this to happen, there must be a reclaiming of the Seven Mountains of Culture in nations. As these spheres are conquered and claimed, nations can begin to shift into their divine image. Each believer is called to operate in at least one of these mountains. Obviously, everyone is not to be in the religion mountain. There are those called to be business people, politicians, educators, artists, newscasters, moms and dads, and other roles in society. Regardless of where we are called to and set, we are not just there to make a living but to also bring reformation in the realm with which we have been trusted. The problem in all of this is the devil would hold legal rights in the spirit to claim these spheres. Remember that only from a legal right can the devil operate according to First Peter 5:8. He devours destinies, substance, dreams, relationships, and all that is valuable because of a legal right he has gained. If we are to see these mountains redeemed and nations shift, we are going to have to take control of them from the Courts of Heaven. The legal rights of the devil must be revoked, and the passion of the kingdom, therefore, set in place from the books of heaven.

When I look at culture as a whole, I understand that it is iniquity in the history of a culture that is allowing the devil to operate. In Second Corinthians 4:3–4, we see Paul speaking about veils being over peoples' hearts and eyes.

> *But even if our gospel is veiled, it is veiled to those who are perishing, whose minds the god of this age has blinded, who do not believe, lest the light of the gospel of the glory of Christ, who is the image of God, should shine on them.*

Paul said the problem is not the presentation of the Gospel of the kingdom. The problem is that the hearts and minds of cultures are veiled by the god of this age. The god of this age is presently in control of each of the Seven Mountains of Culture. I would say these gods are called principalities and powers of the demonic realm in other places in Scripture (see Ephesians 6:12). If we are to see the reformation of culture, we must see the legal right of these entities pulled down from each mountain. Their influence is allowing the mountain to have the worldview it has. Once this god's right is revoked and removed, its influence diminishes. The kingdom believers will have the right and honor of influencing these mountains in accordance with God's heart. The thing that empowers these gods/principalities is the iniquity in the culture of its society. If we are to see each power that is ruling a particular mountain, we must undo the legal right it holds over this sphere through iniquity. This means undoing the sin and iniquity in its history. Allow me to show you a picture of this from Scripture.

Again, I would pinpoint the story of David, Israel, and the Gibeonites. We looked at it earlier from one perspective. I would like to present it in relation to culture and nation. In Second Samuel 21:1–2, we see David discerning why there has been a famine for three years.

> *Now there was a famine in the days of David for three years, year after year; and David inquired of the LORD. And the LORD answered, "It is because of Saul and his bloodthirsty house, because he killed the Gibeonites." So the king called the Gibeonites and spoke to them. Now the Gibeonites were not of the children of Israel, but of the remnant of the Amorites; the children of Israel had sworn protection to them, but Saul had sought to kill them in his zeal for the children of Israel and Judah.*

A whole nation is suffering through a famine because 70 years before Saul had broken a covenant with the Gibeonites. Joshua had made a covenant with them that was binding in heaven. When Saul disregarded it and broke it, the devil had the legal right he was looking for to afflict the whole culture. They could have prayed forever with no results because the devil's legal right was in force. However, once David dealt with the broken covenant and reinstated it, the prayer for the land was heard, and the famine was broken. Second Samuel 21:14 declares the result of David's legal activity on behalf of the land.

> *They buried the bones of Saul and Jonathan his son in the country of Benjamin in Zelah, in the tomb of Kish his father. So they performed all that the king commanded. And after that God heeded the prayer for the land.*

If we are to see our prayers be effective for the land and/ or culture, we must deal with the legal issue satan is using to hold it. Once we repent and ask for the blood to speak on behalf of our nations and cultures, the rights of these principalities that are ruling these mountains can be revoked. In Zechariah 3:9–10, we see an astounding statement concerning that which is stopping the reclamation of cultures and spheres of society.

> *"For behold, the stone*
> *That I have laid before Joshua:*
> *Upon the stone are seven eyes.*
> *Behold, I will engrave its inscription,"*
> *Says the LORD of hosts,*

*"And I will remove the iniquity of that land in one
day.*

*In that day," says the LORD of hosts,
"Everyone will invite his neighbor
Under his vine and under his fig tree."*

Joshua, the High Priest in previous verses, has been
cleaned to stand in his place in the Courts of Heaven.
From this place of judicial activity, God makes a promise.
He declares, "I will remove the iniquity of that land in one
day." When we come before the Lord and repent on behalf
of the land and the mountains we represent and stand in, it
grants the Lord the legal right to *remove the iniquity immedi-
ately.* Once this is done, the legal right of the devil to hold
this sphere of influence can be revoked. When it is removed,
the sphere is now free to be claimed back for the kingdom
of God. The promise of the people inviting neighbors to
their vine and fig tree was a reference to a culture living
in divine order and peace. It was a statement of peace and
prosperity in a culture. God is declaring that once the legal
rights of the devil are revoked because iniquity is removed,
the culture of a nation will come to kingdom order. Wow!
We can step into the Courts of Heaven and take our place
in the sphere we are called to. When we do this, we can
be a part of seeing a culture shift and a nation come to its

divine destiny and purpose. We can see the mountain we are called to be shaped into the mold intended by God.

I would give you one caution as we come before the Lord and His Courts in regards to these realms. We must stay within the jurisdiction we have been given presently. It is one thing to repent on behalf of a culture. It is another to challenge principalities. All of us can repent for the iniquity of the culture we are a part of. Contending with the principalities and powers in the Courts requires a jurisdiction that is relegated to the apostolic. I believe when Paul spoke of wrestling against principalities and powers that he was speaking of himself and his apostolic company (see Ephesians 6:12). I believe that we as believers can be a part of a company repenting and even asking God for mercy and His passion to be done. However, challenging powers of darkness must be left to those who have been called into this sphere. Even then, it must be with an awareness of timing and grace. This is simply my understanding after years of functioning in these dimensions.

Having said all this, here is a prayer you can pray to begin to see the Seven Mountains of Culture shift and be claimed for the kingdom of God.

Lord, as I come before Your Courts, I stand here in the righteousness of God in Christ Jesus. I ask that the blood of Jesus according to Hebrews 12:24 would speak on behalf of my family and myself. I thank You that Your blood is my safeguard and my access to and my justification before You. I ask that the blood would allow me to function here to serve Your will in the nations.

Lord, I come before Your Courts on behalf of the mountain of culture that I represent. (At this point specifically announce the mountain/mountains you feel called to and function in.) Lord, I ask that this mountain might be a representation of Your purpose in the earth. I ask, Lord, that the effect and influence of this mountain over my nation might be in agreement with Your kingdom purpose. Lord, I want all that is written in the books of heaven for my nation to be fleshed out on the earth. May Your will be done on earth even as it is in heaven.

Lord, as I stand before this Court, as one who would represent this mountain, I repent for the mindset, worldview, and rebellion of my mountain. I ask, Lord, that You would forgive us and allow the blood of Jesus to speak for us here. According to

Your Word in Zechariah 3:9-10, would You allow all iniquity that is empowering darkness against Your purposes to be removed in this day. Lord, I thank You for the blood of Jesus that would speak for us and this part of culture. Lord, let this mountain that I represent now be reclaimed for Your will to be done on the earth!

Lord, I am asking that the nations would be claimed for Your will. You, Lord, are worthy of the worship of nations. According to Psalm 2:8, let the nations belong to You. Please, Lord, have for Yourself the nations as Your inheritance and the ends of the earth as Your possession. Lord, they are Yours. Please, Lord, let every other force seeking to claim them be revoked and their rights removed. Lord, let the name of Jesus rule over my mountain and the nations. Lord, I love You. Let Your jealousy over the nations be known. Lord, rule the nations with Your rod of iron according to Revelation 2:27. Lord, You are worthy of all their worship. I stand with You, Lord, shielded by the blood and claim my mountain and the nations for Your purpose. In Jesus's name, Amen.

CHAPTER 15

REVIVAL FROM THE COURTS OF HEAVEN

THE Lord's passion and desire is to see revival and awakening come to the earth. It is the responsibility of the church, however, to give birth to it. I believe this happens from the Courts of Heaven. For many years, it seemed the perspective of the church was we had to convince God to send revival. It seemed God, as a result of our pitiful longing, would finally decide to show mercy and give us a reviving. My perspective, however, has changed. I do not believe we have to convince God to do something He already longs to see happen. I believe we, from the perspective of the Courts of Heaven, must deal with spiritual realties that are stopping the revival from coming. To really understand this, I believe we need to understand the true nature of prayer. Prayer is not trying to convince God to do something. Prayer is stepping into spiritual dimensions with God, and through agreeing with God, we see spiritual realities shift so heaven can invade earth. Through our interaction with the Lord in heavenly places, heaven can be made manifest on the earth. This is what we do in the Courts of Heaven. Through our interaction with the Lord and these heavenly dimensions, we get to be a part of the process of God reclaiming the earth back to Himself.

When I speak of revival, I feel I should define it. Real revival is about the church functioning as God's representative on the earth. The result of this is people are born again and turned back to God. The end effect is a reformation of culture that we talked about in the last chapter. Isaiah 43:18–21 gives us a view of revival and the reformation it can and should produce.

> *Do not remember the former things,*
> *Nor consider the things of old.*
>
> *Behold, I will do a new thing,*
> *Now it shall spring forth;*
> *Shall you not know it?*
> *I will even make a road in the wilderness*
> *And rivers in the desert.*

The beast of the field will honor Me,
The jackals and the ostriches,
Because I give waters in the wilderness
And rivers in the desert,
To give drink to My people, My chosen.

This people I have formed for Myself;
They shall declare My praise.

In these verses, we see God promise to do a new thing. The question is, will we be so steeped in the old that we can't recognize the new? He then begins to speak of a road in the wilderness and a river in the desert. He promises to give the beast of the field drink. A river and a road have two things in common. They both go somewhere. They have a destination. A road is a road because it leads you to a place. This is why people travel roads. A river also goes somewhere. Ultimately it ends up in the sea or ocean. The other commonality is a road has shoulders, while a river has banks. Both of these determine the direction they go. God is faithful to send outpouring/revivals. Without banks on a river, the outpouring becomes a flood that goes nowhere. However, when there are banks, this flood becomes a river. The banks of an outpouring/revival are the apostolic and prophetic. Through these two gifts, there is the ability to discern and give direction and stewardship to the outpourings of God. Historically, when outpouring or revival has come, there hasn't been much stewardship of them. In these days though, the revivals, outpouring, and awakenings of God will be directed and led by apostles and prophets. These people will have been trained, seasoned, and mentored by the Lord for such a time as this. They will have been uniquely shaped and formed to give guidance to these awesome and tremendous moves of God. Notice that the jackals, ostriches, and beast of the field honor the Lord. It doesn't say they all get saved. It says they will have a respect for the Lord and His ways. These speak of unredeemed culture. Even though they may not become followers of Jesus, the effect of His presence in culture will cause them to revere Him. Culture will shift because of the revival of the Lord. The other thing that should be noticed is the thing that birthed all of this was the thirst of God's people. God rises to give His people drink. This is what births revival that ultimately transforms culture. The cry of God's people touches His heart and causes things to be rearranged in the spirit for the outpouring of glory to come.

Another place where we see revival coming and power being displayed that shifts a culture is Elijah on Mount Carmel. In First Kings 18:30–40, after it hasn't rained for over three years, Elijah confronts the prophets of Baal. The result was a display of God's power that began to turn the heart of a culture back to God—in other words, a revival.

Then Elijah said to all the people, "Come near to me." So all the people came near to him. And he repaired the altar of the LORD that was broken down. And Elijah took twelve stones, according to the number of the tribes of the sons of Jacob, to whom the word of the LORD had come, saying, "Israel shall be your name." Then with the stones he built an altar in the name of the LORD; and he made a trench around the altar large enough to hold two seahs of seed. And he put the wood in order, cut the bull in pieces, and laid it on the wood, and said, "Fill four waterpots with water, and pour it on the burnt sacrifice and on the wood." Then he said, "Do it a second time," and they did it a second time; and he said, "Do it a third time," and they did it a third time. So the water ran all around the altar; and he also filled the trench with water.

And it came to pass, at the time of the offering of the evening sacrifice, that Elijah the prophet came near and said, "LORD God of Abraham, Isaac, and Israel, let it be known this day that You are God in Israel and I am Your servant, and that I have done

> *all these things at Your word. Hear me, O LORD, hear me, that this people may know that You are the LORD God, and that You have turned their hearts back to You again."*
>
> *Then the fire of the LORD fell and consumed the burnt sacrifice, and the wood and the stones and the dust, and it licked up the water that was in the trench. Now when all the people saw it, they fell on their faces; and they said, "The LORD, He is God! The LORD, He is God!"*
>
> *And Elijah said to them, "Seize the prophets of Baal! Do not let one of them escape!" So they seized them; and Elijah brought them down to the Brook Kishon and executed them there.*

Elijah in this scenario was presenting a case before the Lord in the Courts of Heaven. He actually was reestablishing the trading floors in the Courts of Heaven. The result was a manifestation of power that broke the hardened hearts of a culture. The people fell on their face and cried, "The Lord He is God, The Lord He is God." This happened because of Elijah's actions on the trading floors of the Courts of Heaven. Notice what Elijah did. First, he called the people close to him. He wasn't beckoning them to come get a better view. He was inviting them into the spiritual dimension of the Courts of Heaven with him. These people would represent the whole of Israel before the Lord. Elijah then rebuilds the altar with 12 stones that represented the 12 tribes of Israel. Elijah was reminding God of the covenant He had with Israel. Even though Israel was not worthy of God's grace, Elijah understood the covenant-keeping nature of God. That what He might not do because they deserved it, He would do because of who He is. Once the altar was rebuilt, Elijah then put the offering of the bull cut into pieces on the altar. This action declared that the people laid themselves on the altar before Him. Every piece of them they give to Him. Then they filled the trench they had dug with water. This was the trade they were making. Water was the most valuable thing they had. It had not rained for over three years. On the basis of all this that was done, Elijah then made a petition to God as he stood before His Courts on the trading floors. He asked, "Lord let it be known there is a God in Israel." He declared, "Let it be known I am Your servant." Then He added, "Let it be known I have done these things at Your word." The fire of God then fell from heaven and the people fell on their face at this display!

Elijah made his request once the trading floors were reestablished in the Courts of Heaven before the Lord. If we desire revival, may we, too, reestablish any altars/trading floors that have fallen down. May we remind God of His covenant with us by the blood of Jesus. May we lay ourselves without reservation on His altar in complete surrender. May every piece of us be yielded to the Lord. May we extravagantly stand on this now established trading floor and offer that which is precious to us. As it is received not just in the earthly realm but also in the heavenly realm of His Courts, may fire fall from heaven and turn our hearts back to Him. Lord, we cry for revival in our land as You hear our petition before Your Courts.

Lord, as we come to stand before Your Courts, we cry for revival in our land. We ask, Lord, that You would hear our petition. We desire to see an outpouring of Your glory that would turn our calloused hearts back to You. Would You cause a river to run in the deserts that would make glad the people of God, but also cause an unredeemed culture to honor You. Lord, we need You and Your glory to touch us and our nations. Please, Lord, pour out Your Spirit on us again.

Lord, we remind You of the covenant we have with You through the blood of Jesus. Lord, we are

Your people. We ask that You would remember us because of the blood speaking on our behalf. We come, Lord, to lay our life down before You. As best we know how, we lay every piece of us on the altar. We hold nothing back. We bring an offering before You that we ask might be accepted. We also bring anything You might require or ask of us. With delight we take what is precious and offer it before You. Let this trade speak before You just as the water in Elijah's day spoke before You.

Lord, now on the basis of this, as Elijah asked of You, so I ask of You. Would You let it be known that You are God in heaven and over us. Would You let it be known, Lord, that we are Your servants. Would You let it be known that we have honored Your word. Lord, I ask that Your fire would fall from heaven and consume our sacrifice. Would You send revival to our land and turn our hearts again to You. Would You from Your Courts allow Your glory to be known and Your power to flow again in the nations. Lord, we ask that this might be done for Your honor and praise. We promise, Lord, to steward correctly with Your help this outpouring that will change nations. Thank You, Lord, for Your tender mercies coming to us from

Your Courts and trading floors of heaven. We love You, Lord. Thanks for Your kindness toward us. In Jesus's name, Amen.

ROBERT HENDERSON is a global, apostolic leader who operates in revelation and impartation. His teaching empowers the body of Christ to see the hidden truths of Scripture clearly and apply them for breakthrough results. Driven by a mandate to disciple nations through writing and speaking, Robert travels extensively around the globe, teaching on the apostolic, the Kingdom of God, the "Seven Mountains," and most notably, the Courts of Heaven. He has been married to Mary for 40 years. They have six children and five grandchildren. Together they are enjoying life in beautiful Midlothian, TX.

INCREASE THE EFFECTIVENESS OF YOUR PRAYERS.

Learn how to release your destiny from Heaven's Courts!

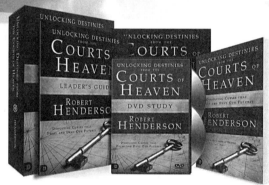

Unlocking Destinies from the Courts of Heaven
Curriculum Box Set Includes:
9 Video Teaching Sessions (2 DVD Disks), Unlocking Destinies *book,*
Interactive Manual, Leader's Guide

There are books in Heaven that record your destiny and purpose. Their pages describe the very reason you were placed on the Earth.

And yet, there is a war against your destiny being fulfilled. Your archenemy, the devil, knows that as you occupy your divine assignment, by default, the powers of darkness are demolished. Heaven comes to Earth as God's people fulfill their Kingdom callings!

In the *Unlocking Destinies from the Courts of Heaven* book and curriculum, Robert Henderson takes you step by step through a prophetic prayer strategy. By watching the powerful video sessions and going through the Courts of Heaven process using the interactive manual, you will learn how to dissolve the delays and hindrances to your destiny being fulfilled.

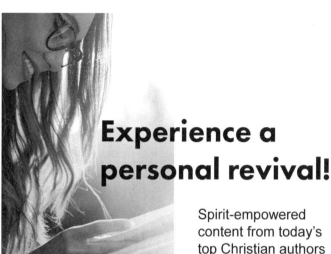